Jack the Ripper

–

Codes lead to Germany

Thomas Hattemer

Jack the Ripper
–
Codes lead to Germany

Bibliografische Information der Deutschen Nationalbibliothek
Die Deutsche Nationalbibliothek verzeichnet diese Publikation
in der Deutschen Nationalbibliografie; detaillierte bibliografische
Daten sind im Internet über http://dnb.d-nb.de abrufbar.

© 2021 Thomas Hattemer
Grafik Covergestaltung: GrayWallStudio/ Denis Simonov/
Shutterstock.com
Covergestaltung, Herstellung und Verlag:
BoD - Books on Demand, Norderstedt
ISBN 978-3-7543-3623-6

Contents

#1 RIPPER FEIGENBAUM IN LONDON   **14**

His sister née Zahn in the Ann Arbor Register   14

His brother John Zahn one day before execution   14

Hatred of women   15

Interview, whether in London in 1888   15

Lawyer Lawton: "in fact Jack the Ripper"   15

Personal description   16

His victim in the USA 1894   17

Execution of Feigenbaum 1896   19

#2 SERIAL KILLER NUMBER 2   **21**

Home address - only 8 km away from Anton Zahn   21

Johann Otto Hoch is Johann Schmitt   21

Number of murders of the Horrweiler: 19   22

Forsaken women of the Horrweilers: 22   24

Aliasnames of Johann Schmitt   26

Robbed Women – US-Dollar   27

Arrested in 1905 and executed in 1906   28

Summary and mentality   29

#3 CODINGS SOLVE THE MYSTERY   **32**

JACK THE RIPPER CRIME SCENES – CODES   **36**

Crooked cross - the performers?   36

Street names - the client?   37

Names of the murdered women - the motive?   39

TRACES REAL OR DECEPTION?   **43**

CRIME SCENES - CALCULATION (ANGLE)   **44**

Leaning Cross - intersection in London   44

Leaning cross-angles in London 93.82°   46

NUMEROLOGY   **50**

First and Last Name of the nobleman 4 & 4 = 8   50

Only "nine" (german: neun) results again = 9   51

Bury = 3 – the only English word   52

ANGLE - LIKE IN LONDON – 93.83°   **53**

Distance 2 degrees of latitude and longitude   53

Gau-Bickelheim–Horrweiler–Pf.-Schwabenheim   54

GAME WITH 6 / 60 / 600 KILOMETERS   **58**

Gau-Bickelheim – Pfaffen-Schwabenheim: 6 km   58

Pfaffen-Schwabenheim – Frankfurt: 60 km   58

Pfaffen-Schwabenheim – Koblenz: 60 km   59

Whitechapel – Gau-Bickelheim: 600 km   60

GERMAN NOBLEMAN IN LONDON CODE   63

MOTIVE - DUEL IN FREIBURG 1888?   65

Death at 22, grandson of Kaiser Wilhelm I.   65

Officially pneumonia   66

"Honor of the sister"   68

Indirect witness Graf von Baudissin   68

Swear vengeance on deathbed?   69

Possible opponent in a possible duel   69

William Hamilton: Too far fetched?   70

Fit for duel over UK school and sport?   70

Sister - reason for possible duel?   71

Older line Baden & Divorce from Monaco   72

Father – 11. Duke of Hamilton   72

Often in Baden and Paris   73

Second husband of the sister   73

Until 1888 in Baden-Baden   74

Mother – Marie Amelie von Baden   74

Death October 1888, Kaspar Hauser   75

Common ancestor of Hamilton and Baden 76

Palace Hamilton near Glasgow in Scotland 76

BISMARCK'S WORK WITH LONDON 77

1882-84 on site & "à distance" until 1889 77

Character of Herbert von Bismarck 77

Revenge for insult? 78

CYNICAL PUN 79

"The cross follows" (>90°) – (Bad) Kreuznach 79

Bismarck – "Biß ins Mark" OR "bis ins Mark" 79

JAKOB KOETH III. (1850-1904) 80

Evidence of involvement in murders 80

Builder 1888 house in Pfaffen-Schwabenheim 81

Johann Eibach records death – his relatives 82

Campaign 1870/71 war memorial 83

Administrator of the village treasury (collector) 83

Death "abroad" only in the register Aug./Sept. 1904 84

Wife's suicide March 17, 1945 - US Army invades 86

The heirs of the house and the mayors 87

Lots of Köth's in village - wine dealers 88

Niece's relationships with the bishop 88

1+8+8+8 KM AIR LINE 89

Lonsheim_Gau-Bickelheim_Horrweiler_Bingen 89

WHOM BISMARCK KNOWS NEAR KOETH 94

KNOWS BISMARCK - NEAR KOETH 96

Albrecht von Stosch (1818–1896) 96

Heinrich Eduard v. Lade (1817–1904) 98

Ludwig Bamberger (1823–1899) 101

WHO DID THE CALCULATIONS? 102

Kaiserliche Admiralität 102

Kartographisches Amt (military) 104

1888 STUTTGART – 2. KILLER IN USA? 105

Lover Charles Woodcock (bis 1888) 105

Reason for the murders of Johann Hoch? 106

Charles Woodcock was 38 years old in 1888 106

Numerology: Charles = 3 & Woodcock = 8 106

King Karl I. von Württemberg 107

Prime Minister Mittnacht 109

300000 / 30000 / 3000 Reichsmark 111

Stuttgart – Chicago: 7077 km air line 111

MAXIMUM VARIATION ANGLE 93,82°   112

Axis Mitre Square to Buck's Row fixed   112

Axis Hanbury St. to Berner St. variable   112

Reason for Hanbury number 29 = 1888 House   116

PLANNING IN LONDON   118

Selection of the storage locations for the corpses   118

Selection of women based on their names   118

Selection of killers for London and USA   119

Calculation of 1+8+8+8 km, who?   120

Choice of days for the murders   120

Site inspection in London   121

CITY MAP LONDON 1888 AND MURDERS   123

FAMILY OF ANTON ZAHN 1789 TO 1840   124

Grandparents, aunts, uncles, bases, cousins   124

Conflict aunt, father   126

Two cousins weddings 1840   126

Discarded emigration 1840   127

ANTON ZAHN – CHILDHOOD   134

Birth 1841 in Gau-Bickelheim   134

Church demolished in 1842 and rebuilt 1853   134

Condemnation of the brother Carl 1846 in Mainz   135

Aunt emigrates to the USA with her son   139

Confirmation by Bishop Ketteler 1853   142

Death of the father in 1855   144

ANTON ZAHN – IN PRISON   **145**

Penitentiary for theft 1863-1868   145

Prison near Maria Dolorosa & brothel district   147

Acquaintances in prison   149

ANTON ZAHN – FROM 1869   **151**

At his aunt's funeral in USA 1869?   151

Death of mother in 1876 in Gau-Bickelheim   151

ANTON ZAHN – 1888 IN LONDON?   **152**

Jack the Rippers victims in London   152

First murder   154

Markus Adam Nickel & Mary Ann Nichols   155

DISAPPEARED DOCUMENTS   **163**

Crew lists of 1888 in Bremen   163

Court minutes Okt. 1863 in Mainz   163

Conjectures about Anton Zahn's theft   166

ANTON ZAHN – FROM 1892 IN USA   169

Resident in Syracuse 1892   169

Heritage in Cincinnati 1894   171

ANTON ZAHN – AGAIN TO 1894/96   173

Parents - 9 instead of 3 siblings   173

Interview of his brother Johann Zahn   176

Game of Anton Zahn with names   178

Appearance of Anton Zahn 1894 to 1896   178

Inner urge to kill women   179

Always a deep, gloomy mood   181

INGELHEIM IN 1860 – OTTO HOCH WAS 5   183

FEIGENBAUM   186

The real Carl Feigenbaum (*1841; 1910 in prison)   186

Fig tree cursed by Jesus   189

SKETCHES OF ANGLES AND DISTANCES   191

Angle in London 1888   191

London angle in Rheinhessen   192

Bingen to Lonsheim 1+8+8+8 km   193

Angle between Arran, Berlin, "Carlsruhe" (ABC)   194

Extension to Stuttgart   195

Extension to Kaiserslautern   196

Extension to Bonn   197

Hanbury 29 identified from location 1888 house   198

60 km to Koblenz and Frankfurt   199

600 km to London – 6 km to 1888 house   200

DOCUMENTS ABOUT ZAHN   **201**

NOTES ON JACOB KOETH III.   **206**

LIST OF REFERENCES   **208**

Television and books   208

Internet   210

LIST OF ILLUSTRATIONS (ON PAGE 192)   **225**

#1 Ripper Feigenbaum in London

His sister née Zahn in the Ann Arbor Register

Carl Ferdinand Feigenbaum, suspected of being Jack the Ripper, had two attorneys for his defense, Hugh O. Pentecost and William Stamford Lawton. Attorney Lawton had a residence in the city of Ann Arbor, located about 35 miles west of Detroit.

From there Lawton arranged to give the inheritance of the executed man in New York in 1896 to his sister Margarethe Strohband, née Zahn. This sister lived in Gau-Bickelheim, district of Alzey, Rheinhessen, at that time belonging to the Grand Duchy of Hesse-Darmstadt. (Wolf Vanderlinden: www.casebook.org/suspects/carl-feigenbaum.html)

These documents of Lawton from Ann Arbor are a decisive source to the fact that Carl Feigenbaum came from Gau-Bickelheim and was actually called **Anton Zahn**.

The date of his birth is in the church register: May 17, 1841.

His brother John Zahn one day before execution

His brother John or Johann Zahn, who at that time lived with his family in Brooklyn (borough of New York) and had already immigrated in 1855, had visited the death row inmate Carl Feigenbaum one day before his execution and then confirmed to the press that Anton had immigrated to the USA in 1892 and had previously been a sailor. This is further proof of his actual surname Zahn (and not Feigenbaum).

Hatred of women

Anton Zahn recounts during his time in New York prison:
"I have for years suffered from a singular disease, which induces an all-absorbing passion. This passion manifests itself in a desire to kill and mutilate the woman who falls in my way. At such times I am unable to control myself."

Interview, whether in London in 1888

By the time he was executed in the electric chair in April 1896 at Sing Sing prison north of New York on the Hudson River (the West Point military academy is also nearby), his lawyer Lawton had the opportunity to get to know his client.
When asked if he was responsible for the murders in Whitechapel, London in 1888, Anton Zahn replied that "only Lord knows."

Lawyer Lawton: "in fact Jack the Ripper"

Carl Feigenbaum's lawyer William Sanford Lawton gave an interview to a reporter from the New York Advertiser newspaper shortly after the execution. In it, the lawyer expressed his belief that his ex-client was in fact the notorious Jack the Ripper.

The Advertiser broke the news, and the sensation was then printed in many newspapers in North America. The world, however, had many other difficult tasks to deal with and the story was quickly forgotten.

Lawyer Lawton told the press that he assumed that his client, whose life he could not save, admitted to having been in London at the times in question in 1888. Moreover, he said, before immigrating to the U.S. in 1892, he had been a sailor (with the special duty of fighting fires) on ships of North German Lloyd.

Personal description

Newspaper accounts at the time, such as the Daily Republican from Decatur in the U.S. state of Illinois, show a drawing in side profile of Anton Zahn, alias Carl Feigenbaum. It shows a well-dressed, serious-looking, older man (between 45 and 50) with a quiff of hair and a small upper lip beard and a narrow little fuzz under his lower lip. His face shows a mixture of exhaustion, cruelty, frustration, adventurousness and austerity, but also calmness, intelligence and gentility.

A photograph - taken when he was committed to Sing Sing Prison - was unfortunately destroyed along with many other documents 75 years later (i.e., around 1972), according to regulations. Only the committal form of the "Sing Sing" Correctional Facility from 1895 survived the destruction unharmed.

There, under the name "Carl Feigenbaum", the inmate is described as: Born – Germany
- Age – 54
- Married – (not specified)
- Occupation – Florist
- Height – 5.4 ins (1 meter 62.6 cm)
- Weight – 126 lbs (57.15 kilogram)
- Religion – Catholic
- Complexion – medium

5.4 ins have to be read as 5 feet and 4 inches.
1 foot is 30,48 cm and 1 inch is 2.54 cm.
1 foot = 12 inches.
1 lb = 453.6 gram

His victim in the USA 1894

Juliana Hoffman in New York, Sept. 1, 1894.

In the murder of Juliana Hoffman, an immigrant from Hungary who lives with her 16-year-old son in a small apartment, a man can be apprehended who at first claims to be "Carl Feigenbaum".

The woman had sublet a room to the florist Anton Zahn on August 29, 1894, because, like many immigrants, she urgently needed money. At first even without advance payment, because Zahn pretended not to have any money yet, which was not true.

According to his statements, Anton Zahn had lost his job as a gardener on Long Island in late July, early August 1894. He would have moved around the country, taking all sorts of cheap jobs and last sleeping on a park bench in Tompkins Square Park, a block from Mrs. Hoffman's apartment.

On the night of the murder, he would have waited until Mrs. Hoffman fell asleep, then put an end to the poor woman by strangling her and cutting her throat. However, because Mrs. Hoffman had woken up frightened, there was still a small fight, and from his mother's screaming also her son, 16-year-old Michael, woke up.

At first he wanted to help his mother. Then, when he realized that he had no chance against Anton Zahn, who was 53 years old at the time, and was also attacked by him with a knife, the boy jumped out of the window and escaped down the fire escape via the inner courtyard onto the street, where he made such a ruckus that the men, who were still out so late, were able to grab the murderer by the arms.

Earlier, Anton Zahn had tried to wash the blood off his hands in the courtyard, which did not quite succeed in the rush. The police also arrived quickly, returned to the scene

17

with the boy and the man they had caught, and then arrested Carl Feigenbaum.

The police found the murderer's bag, in which the 15cm long knife fit. Also inside was a sharpening stone to keep the blade at an exceptionally sharp edge on a regular basis.

At first Zahn claimed that his friend Jakob Weibel had committed the crime. The victim's child, however, repeatedly and emphatically confirmed that Anton Zahn was the perpetrator. Now, in addition, after numerous interrogations in prison, he was suspected of being "Jack the Ripper" or at least one of the "most promising" candidates.

The website www.jack-the-ripper.org gives the address of the murder under the keyword "Carl Feigenbaum":

New York, 544 East 6th Street

House No. 544 - just before the intersection with Avenue B - has been demolished (like the neighboring house to the west, No. 542, and the neighboring houses to the east, No. 92, etc.). The district is called "Alphabet City." It was also known as "Little Germany" in the 2nd half of the 19th century. The parent borough is called "East Village." (Wikipedia)

Tompkins Square Park is located on the southeast side of Manhattan Island, 2.7 km north-northeast to the Brooklyn Brigde, between

In the North:	East 10th Street
In the South:	East 7th Street
In the West:	Avenue A
In the East:	Avenue B

So the house where Juliana Hoffman was stabbed was one block south of the above park. (see on Google Maps)

Execution of Feigenbaum 1896

Anton Zahn alias Carl Feigenbaum was executed in the electric chair on April 27, 1896 in the "Sing Sing" prison in Ossining, Westchester County, New York State, USA.

He spent his last night on earth together with the prison priest "Father" Creeden. With him was "Father" Bruder from the Catholic Church in the small village of Poughkeepsie, also located north of Ossining on the Hudson River. There, far and wide, was the only Catholic cemetery where Anton Zahn was buried under the name Carl Feigenbaum. Zahn had $90 ready for just that. As a typical loner, he was poorly dressed, but probably had quite a bit of wealth.

One of the Fathers gave him his last rites before his last breakfast on the morning of April 27. Also before this last meal, he thereby announced his last will and testament before the priests and before the prison authorities.

Feigenbaum directed in his orally presented will that his house and another apartment in the city of Cincinnati in the state of Ohio be sold, and the proceeds, along with his money in a bank in New York, be bequeathed to his sister Magdalena widowed Strohband in Gau-Bickelheim, Alzey, Hesse-Darmstadt, Germany, in addition to the $90 for his grave.

Anton Zahn was one of the first people to be executed in an electric chair. The first in the world was a Mr. William Kemmler on August 6, 1890, and the chair was first introduced in New York State. This was because a senator had observed a man die instantly when he fell on a high-voltage cable. As a result, this electric chair killing method was developed. However, in the case of the first death candidate Kemmler, it had only been tried with 1000 volts, which was too little.

The researcher Wolf Vanderlinden quotes the day of execution as follows: Omar Van Leuven Sage, then warden of the prison, took charge of the execution. At 11:10 on Monday morning, April 27, 1896 Zahn was told that his time had come. Accompanied by the two priests, he was led from his cell to the execution room.

Before sitting down on the uncomfortable wooden chair, he kissed the crucifix he had with him and handed it to Father Bruder. Without haste, he sat down on the electric chair. Then he took off his glasses and gave them to Father Brother with the request to bury the glasses together with him. While the straps were fastened on him he kissed the hand of Warden Sage, shook the hands of both Pastors Creeden and Bruder, and likewise that of State Electrician Davis, who would kill him.

The prisoner was quickly secured in the chair. Electrodes were fixed to the top of his head and to the ankle of his left leg. Then after the prison physician Dr. R.T. Irvine gave the OK, Warden told Davis to turn on the electricity.

The first electric shock of 1820 volts was given at 11:16 a.m. and lasted 30 seconds. It was then gradually lowered to 300 volts. It was then held at 300 volts for 40 seconds. After the current was turned off for a few seconds, a second surge of 1820 volts, also at 11:17 a.m., was run through the body and held for 15 seconds until exactly 11:18 a.m. Drs. Irvine and John Wilson Gibbs, who monitored the duration and voltages, examined the body and pronounced Anton Zahn dead at 11:19.

At least the Fort Wayne News newspaper reported that two other medical examiners were called in to investigate whether Anton Zahn was indeed dead. Because of the uncertainty of one or two of the four doctors, it was decided to run electricity through the body again to be absolutely sure. Full voltage was maintained for a period of 3 seconds at about 21:25. After that, the deceased was declared really dead.

#2 Serial killer number 2

Home address - only 8 km away from Anton Zahn

2 German serial killers were on the loose from 1888:

- Anton Zahn in London, presumably "Jack the Ripper".
- Joh. Schmitt in/around Chicago. "Bluebeard Murderer"

Astonishing: They lived only 8 km apart in Germany.
Otto Hoch alias Johann Schmitt lived in Horrweiler, Anton Zahn alias Carl Feigenbaum came from Gau-Bickelheim. Horrweiler is 8 km north of Gau-Bickelheim.

Both are executed in the USA, 1896 and 1906.

Johann Otto Hoch is Johann Schmitt

Johann Schmitt is married to a Christine née Ramb in Horrweiler. With her he has three children. In 1887 he leaves his wife behind in Rheinhessen.

From 1888 and especially between 1892 and 1901, Otto Hoch murders and cheats on countless women around Chicago.

Before emigrating to the USA, Johann Schmitt alias Johann Otto Hoch is also said to have stayed in Austria, France and Great Britain.

Number of murders of the Horrweiler: 19

He committed the following murders of 19 women:

In 1881, Schmitt married an Annie Hock in Austria. At that time, however, he was still married to his wife Christine née Ramb in Horrweiler until 1887.

1) 1883, New York - Schmitt arrives in New York with his wife Annie Hock, a disabled woman who dies years later.
2) 1888, New York - Arrives in New York via Württemberg (Germany). He discloses that he is married to a waitress who died two months earlier.
3) 1892, Chicago - Mrs. Hoyle Hoch dies. Then Johann Schmitt from Horrweiler takes her family name. (There is also Hoch family in Rheinhessen).
4) May 1892, Chicago - Johann Schmitt takes the name C.A. Meyer. He rents an apartment and has a new wife. She dies after three weeks.
5) June 1892, Chicago - Johann Schmitt takes the name H. Irick, rents an apartment again and has a new wife. She dies a month later.
6) 1893, Milwaukee - Schmitt is now called "Dr. James" and marries Lena Schmitz. She dies.
7) 1893, Milwaukee - Schmitt marries sister Clara. She too presumably dies.
8) 1894, Chicago - Under a new name, Schmitt rents an apartment with a new wife. She dies after two months.

After all the murders, from 1895 on, there are also cases where Johann Schmitt "only" leaves the women. He often cheats them out of their money. But more about that in the next chapter.

9) April 1895 - Johann Schmitt marries under the name Jacob Huff a Karoline née Miller, widowed Hoch. She died on June 15, 1895. He faked his death, took the last name "Hoch" with her as well (see 1892) and went back to Chicago, arriving on July 5.

10) August 5, 1895, Chicago - Johann Schmitt married a Maria Steimbucher under the name Jacob Hoch. She died four months later. Schmitt sold her property for $4000. Before her death, she made a statement that she had been poisoned. But the authorities did not take note of this statement.

It is reported that Johann Schmitt fled to Germany (under his real name) between November 1895 and April 1896 because the justice system in the United States was after him for "warrant charging." He had declared himself bankrupt. In Germany he inherited 3000 marks.

In April 1896 Anton Zahn alias Carl Feigenbaum was executed in New York. Perhaps a strange coincidence in time.

11) Sept. 22, 1896, San Francisco - Under his real name Schmitt, he marries the widow Barbara Brossett. He disappears two days later with her $1465. She is so upset by this loss that she dies a short time later.

12) Nov. 1896, Cincinnati (Ohio) - Under the name Hoch, he marries Clara Bartel. She dies three months later.

13) March 1898, Chicago - Under the name Martin Dotz, Johann Schmitt marries a woman who dies in June 1898.

14) 1899, Milwaukee - Schmitt marries a sister of Mrs. J.H. Schwartz-Marue. The bride dies. Schmitt goes into hiding with $1200.

15) 1899, Norfolk (Virginia) - A Mrs. Hoch dies suddenly.

16) 1900, Argos (Indiana) - Under the name Albert Buschberg, he marries a Mary Schultz. Both the wife and her

15 years old daughter Nettie and $2000 have disappeared without a trace.

17) 1901, San Francisco - Johann Schmitt takes Mrs. Loughken. She dies "suddenly."

18) June 1904, Milwaukee - Under the name Hoch, Schmitt marries a Lena Hoch. She dies three weeks after leaving him $1500.

19) Dec. 10, 1904, Chicago - Johann Schmitt marries a Marie Walcker under the name Johann Otto Hoch. She sells her store for the marriage for $7500 and gives the husband $350 from insurance. On December 20, 1904, Maria Walcker becomes ill. On January 12, 1905 she dies.

Forsaken women of the Horrweilers: 22

1) Johann Schmitt is imprisoned in Chicago in 1895 under the name "C.A. Calford" and reported by Mrs. Janet Spencer. He had married her and then left her again. In the process he stole several hundred dollars from the woman.

2) In Nov. 1895, Schmitt married a Mary Rankin in Chicago under the name Hoch. The next day he had already disappeared with her money.

3) In April 1896, Johann Schmitt married a Mary Hartzfield in Chicago under the name Jacob Erdorf. She survived him when he disappeared with her $600 four months later.

4) In January 1897, Johann Schmitt married Julia Dose of Hamilton in Cincinnati, Ohio. One day he disappears with $700, part of her money.

5) On July 20, 1897, he remarries under the name Henry F. Hartman in Cincinnati.

6) On December 6, 1897, he ties the knot again in Williamsburg, New York State. He goes into hiding with a looted $200.

7) On January 16, 1898, the next wedding is scheduled. This time it is Winnie Westphal, whom he marries in Jersey City

under the name William Frederick Bessing. He takes off with $900.

8) In 1900, as Jacob Hoch, he marries an Anna Scheffries in Chicago.

9) Then, on Dec. 20, 1900, he marries an Amelia Hohn of Chicago as John Healy. He robs her of $100 and leaves her.

10) In January 1901, he marries as Carl Schmidt in Columbus, Ohio. He leaves his wife after two weeks with $400 in his pocket.

11) In Nov. 1901 he marries Anna Goehrke. He leaves her.

12) On April 8, 1902, he marries Mary Becker in St. Louis. However, she does not die until 1903, when he had long since left her.

13) In May 1902, Schmitt married a woman named Hulda Nagel under the name Count Otto van Kern. He persuades his wife to turn items into cash. When the woman is out shopping, he breaks open her safe and takes off with $3000. She survives.

14) On June 18, 1903, Schmitt, using the name Dr. G.L. Hart, flees away from Mabel Leichmann, whom he had married three days earlier. He had tried to poison the woman. She survived, but he escaped with $300 worth of diamonds and $200 cash.

15) In 1903, he marries Annie Dold.

16) In 1903, he marries Regina Miller Curtis of Dayton, Ohio.

17) In 1903 he marries Ida Zazuil from Milwaukee.

He leaves all these 3 women again without robbing or killing them.

18) In Dec. 1903 he marries T. O'Connor in Milwaukee. He robs her of $200.

19) Under the name John Jacob Adolf Schmidt, he marries an Anna Hendrickson of Chicago in Hammond, Indiana, on

Jan. 2, 1904. He runs off with $500 of her money on January 20, 1904.

So from May 1902 to January 1904, he didn't kill any women. Presumably he is a wee bit cautious because he knows the police are on his tail.

20) On Oct. 8, 1904, he marries a Bertha Dolder in Chicago under the name Leo Prager. He disappears after receiving 3500 dollars from her to buy a furniture store.
21) On Oct. 20, 1904, under the name John Schmidt (i.e., his real name), he marries a Caroline Streicher of Philadelphia. He takes off on Oct. 31, 1904.
22) On Jan. 15, 1905, Johann Schmitt remarries under the name Johann Otto Hoch to the sister of his poisoned wife. She is a widow and named Fischer. She lives in Joliet (Illinois). She gives him 750 dollars.

Johann Schmitt flees when he is accused of being a murderer and a swindler.
On January 30, 1905, Schmitt, as Harry Bartels, proposes to his landlady Catherine Kimmerle in New York (City). She refuses the marriage. Johann Schmitt is then arrested by the New York police under the name John Joseph Adolf Hoch, which he gives himself. (Wikipedia)

Aliasnames of Johann Schmitt

Officially, Johann Schmitt from Horrweiler is listed as Johann Otto Hoch in the USA. Accused under this name, he had the following aliases:
The Bluebeard Murderer, C.A.Meyer, H. Ireck, Dr James, Jacob Huff, C.A.Calford, Jacob Hoch, Jacob Erdorff, Schmitt, Bartell, Henry F. Hartman, William Frederick Bessing, Martin Dotz, Adolf Hoch, Martin Dose, Albert Buschberg,

John Healey, Carl Schmidt, Count Otto van Kurn, Dr G. L. Hart, John Jacob Leo Schmidt, Leo Preger, Joseph Hoch, Jacob Hock, Henry Bartells, John Joseph Adolf Hoch, Fred Doess

Robbed Women – US-Dollar

The total amount of stolen money is calculated as follows:

Janet Spencer / 1895 / ~$500
Maria Steimbucher, Chicago / 1895 / $4000
Maria Hartzfield, Chicago / 1896 / $600
Barbara Brossett, San Francisco / 1896 / $1465
Marries Julia Dose of Hamilton Ohio-in Cincinnati / 1897 / $700
in Williamsburg / 1897 / $200
Winnie Westphal in Jersey / 1898 / $900
Sister of J.H. Schwartz-Marue, Milwaukee / 1899 / $1200
Mary Schultz of Argos, Indiana / 1900 / $2000
Amelia Hohn, Chicago / 1900 / $100
in Columbus, Ohio / 1901 / $400
Hulda Nagel / 1902 / $3000
Mabel Leichmann (Diamants) / 1903 / $300
Mabel Leichmann / 1903 / $200
T. O'Conner, Milwaukee / 1903 / $200
Anna Hendrickson, Chicago / 1904 / $500
Lena Hoch from Milwaukee / 1904 / $1500
Bertha Dolder, Chicago / 1904 / $3500
Marie Walker, Chicago / 1904 / $350
Fischer in Joliet / 1905 / $750

SUM: $22365

Arrested in 1905 and executed in 1906

Now it goes then nevertheless with Johann Schmitt from Horrweiler to end, when he brings his new wife on 12 January 1905 with poison to death.

After the great wave of murders from 1892 to 1895 and the cases between 1896 and 1901, there was not another obvious murder until 1905. Between 1901 and 1905, Johann Schmitt had limited himself only to robbing.

But exactly this murder in 1905 will bring him to the gallows in 1906.

As I wrote before:

Dec. 10, 1904, Chicago - Johann Schmitt marries a Marie Walcker under the name Johann Otto Hoch. She sells her store for the marriage for $7500 and gives the husband $350 from the insurance. On December 20, 1904, Maria Walcker becomes ill. On January 12, 1905 she dies.

On January 15, Johann Schmitt remarries under the name Johann Otto Hoch to the sister of his poisoned wife. She is a widow and named Fischer. She lives in Joliet (Illinois). She gives him 750 dollars.

Johann Schmitt flees when he is accused of being a murderer and a swindler.

On January 30, 1905, Schmitt, as Harry Bartels, proposes to his landlady Catherine Kimmerle in New York (City). She refuses the marriage. Johann Schmitt is then arrested by the New York police under the name John Joseph Adolf Hoch, which he gives himself.

On February 1, 1905, he is charged with bigamy (multiple marriages). There are 29 women who confirm this.

On February 5, 1905, another five abandoned women are able to confirm Johann Schmitt's identity.

On May 19, 1905, Johann Schmitt is found guilty by the court of having killed Marie Walcker and is sentenced to death in New York on June 23, 1905.

On the same day, because of a matter with a Cora Wilson in Chicago, his case can be transferred to Chicago. The court (Supreme Court Illinois) there sets the date of his execution for August 25, 1905.

On August 25, 1905, the execution is postponed until October. On December 16, 1905, the Illinois Supreme Court denies a retrial.

On February 23, 1906, Johann Schmitt (or Schmidt) is executed under the name Johann Otto Hoch. After his execution by hanging, numerous cemeteries refused to bury him.

Finally, his body was lowered into the ground at Cook County Cemetery. The Chicago State Hospital was later built nearby.

Summary and mentality

It is believed that Johann Schmitt (or: Schmidt) committed about 20 murders between 1890 and 1905. However, there could have been up to just over 50.

Schmitt sometimes took the surnames of his killed wives, but this was not always the case, and sometimes he even used his real name.

The murder of Caroline Hoch is particularly well documented. In February 1895, he appeared as Jacob Huff in the town of Wheeling in the U.S. state of West Virginia. There he won the heart and hand of Caroline Hoch. They married in April, and the wife became seriously ill three months later.

The insidious poisoning by arsenic (and similar substances) over a period of weeks by her husband was even observed "live" with great suspicion in this case by Reverend Hermann Haas during a visit to the "Huffs" in Wheeling. He noticed that after her husband had given her some powder from a small jar, which obviously must have been poison for the Reverend Haas, the wife felt very bad afterwards.

Nevertheless, the reverend did not intervene. He had only been extraordinarily surprised. Probably the good and loving coaxing of Johann Schmitt to the address of his wife Caroline made the Reverend confused and remain in a state of passivity.

Reverend Haas reported the incident to the police, and Police Inspector George Shippy has since attached himself to the heels of Johann Schmitt. Haas also informed the Inspector of the suspicion of bigamy (multiple marriages).

After his wife's death, he plundered her bank account and sold their house.

When Schmitt's clothes, watch, and a note were found on the banks of the Ohio, Johann Schmitt was suspected to have committed suicide. However, a body was never found.

He had always chosen his victims from personals.

Then Johann Schmitt served time in prison for a year in 1898 for defrauding a furniture dealer.

Meanwhile, the body of Caroline Hoch was exhumed to be examined for arsenic. But all vital organs were missing.

According to the book "The Great Encyclopedia of Serial Killers" by Michael Newton, before about 1900, corpses were often embalmed with arsenic. This made a killing with arsenic difficult if not impossible to detect.

After about 1900, morticians used a liquid to embalm the body that no longer contained arsenic. Now forensic scientists were able to prove that Marie Walcker had been poisoned in Chicago by her husband, Johann Schmitt, and convicted him.

His picture was sent to every major daily newspaper in the United States. In New York City, the boarding house hostess recognized "Henry Bartels" as Johann Schmitt, alias Johann Otto Hoch. He had already asked her to marry him 20 minutes after checking into her boarding house. When he was arrested, the police also found a revolver.

Chicago journalists referred to him as "Bluebeard of the Stockyard" and wrote a great deal of true and untrue detail about his past.

At his trial, Johann Schmitt from Horrweiler (Rheinhessen) whistled and hummed to himself during the prosecution's plea and twiddled his thumbs. He apparently enjoyed his position in the limelight. At the verdict of guilty by hanging, he spoke to the court, "It's over with Johann. It serves me right."

As he mounted the gallows on Feb. 23, 1906, he proclaimed his innocence and declared, "I'm done with this world. I'm through with anybody."

As the trapdoor burst open beneath him, a local reporter sneered, "Yes, Mr. Hoch, but the question remains: How did they finish everyone?" (emphasis on "how").

#3 Codings solve the mystery

Let's list a few points:

Two German serial killers were at work from 1888:

Case 1: one in London, probably "Jack the Ripper".
Case 2: the other in/around Chicago. "Bluebeard Murderer"

They lived only 5 miles (8 km) apart in Germany.
Both are executed in the USA, in 1896 and 1906.

Completely new is the coding aspect (case 1):

a) German **client** in <u>street names</u> in Whitechapel.
b) **motive** in <u>names of the murdered women</u>.

The great acrobatics of coordinates between London or Whitechapel and Southwest Germany can actually only have been controlled by a "higher authority" which could have had its headquarters in Berlin, for example. The angles and distances are no coincidence, but carefully prepared.

Number symbolism & author's calculations:

Angle 93.82° (Case 1)
a) Calculation intersection first 4 murders 1888 in London
b) Exact calculation of the **angle in London**
c) **Proof that same angle exists in Rheinhessen**
d) Angle between Scottish island, Karlsruhe and Berlin

First name and surname of the principal result in each case "4", if numerology is applied. Just like the 4 corners of the crooked cross that covers London. Exactly the same angle on the cross exists between the cemeteries of the 2 serial killers' places of origin and the 1888 house in a 3rd parish where the introducer and financier lived on the "lowest level".

Illustration of the year 1888
a) 1+8+8+8 km as the air line in Rheinhessen (cases 1 & 2)
b) improved model compared to book 2015 (in german)
c) extension of the line to Stuttgart possible (case 2)

Distances (Case 1)
a) distance Whitechapel - Gau-Bickelheim: exactly 600 km
b) Pfaffen-Schwabenheim - Koblenz and Frankfurt: 60 km
c) Pfaffen-Schwabenheim - Gau-Bickelheim: 6 km
d) As the air line Gau-Bickelheim-Pf.-Schwabenheim meets London

The 3 places in Rheinhessen:

Locations of the 2 killers, introducers (see 2015 book)
a) Gau-Bickelheimer responsible for London (case 1)
b) Horrweiler responsible for USA (Chicago) (case 2)
c) Guide from Pfaffen-Schwabenheim (cases 1 & 2).

Determination of reference points in Rheinhessen via angle
a) Pfaffen-Schwabenheim: 1888 house with anchor (1 & 2)
b) Cemetery Gau-Bickelheim (case 1)
c) Cemetery Horrweiler (case 2)

Deaths of the "lowest level"
a) Gau-Bickelheim: electric chair, New York, 1896 (1)
b) Pf.-Schwabenheim: away, German secret service? 1904
c) Horrweiler: Hanging, Chicago, 1906 (2).

The presumed, aristocratic principal dies of liver disease in September 1904 (see 2015 book). He himself may be acting on behalf of two southern German states whose rulers are related to the German emperor. "Related" and "Kaiser" can be read from the names of the first three murdered women in Whitechapel.

Whitechapel – Gau-Bickelheim	600 km
Koblenz & Frankfurt – Pf.-Schwabenheim	60 km
Gau-Bickelheim – Pf.-Schwabenheim	6 km

London Jack the Ripper	?	Feigenbaum, Carl alias Anton Zahn		Prince von Baden/Insult — Death Febr. 88
Angle first 4 murders is =		should say: * Karlsruhe		22 years old. Duel?
= Angle Pfaffen-Schwabenheim/ Horrweiler/ Gau-Bickelhm.		Sister: Gau-Bickelheim, like him too		**Name duelist in women's names of London**

?   ?   ?

Jakob Köth III. 1888 House		Herbert von Bismarck		More conspirators?
Pfaffen-Schwabenheim	?	+ Sept. 1904 **Name in**	?	*v Lade +8.1904 v Stosch?*
murdered? Aug/Sept 1904		**Streets of London!**		*Bamberger? Mittnacht?*

?   ?   ?

Chicago Bluebeard Murderer	!	Joh.Otto Hoch alias Joh. Schmitt Horrweiler		Summer 1888 Stuttgart 300000 Reichsmark to blackmailer C. Woodcock
		into USA via Württemberg		Affair with König Karl I.
		Bingen-Stuttgart		

Stuttgart-Chicago	7077 km
Stuttgart-Milwaukee	7007 km

Jack the Ripper Crime scenes – Codes

Crooked cross - the performers?

The first four Jack the Ripper murders result in a cross with an angle of 93.82°.
To do this, connect a) the first murder in the east with the fourth murder in the west and b) the second murder in the north with the third murder in the south.
The calculation for this is below.

The lines to the murders from the intersection in the center have twice the angle 93.82° and twice the angle 180° minus 93.82° equal 86.18°.

It would now be interesting to find these angles elsewhere in the world if the principal(s) of the murders (or the murderer) wanted to lay a trail to themselves here.

The question at this point is whether to work with large 93.82° or small 86.18°. If one considers the chronological sequence of the murders, then it can be only the angle 93.82°. Because this larger angle lies a) between the 1st and 2nd murder and b) between the 3rd and 4th murder.
3rd and 4th murder took place on the same day. The 2nd murder three weeks before and the 1st murder another week before. The angle 86.18° is found between c) the 2nd and 4th murder and d) between the 1st and 3rd murder.

93.82° is also found in Rheinhessen, between the 1888 house in Pfaffen-Schwabenheim (builder: Jakob Köth III) and the two cemeteries in Horrweiler (killer: Johann Schmitt alias Otto Hoch) and in Gau-Bickelheim (killer: Anton Zahn alias Carl Feigenbaum, possibly Jack the Ripper).

Street names - the client?

The street names of the places where the bodies were found are:

a. **Buck's** Row (Victim: Mary Ann Nichols)
b. **Hanbury** Street (Victim: Annie Chapman)
c. **Berner** Street (Victim: Elizabeth Stride) [Dutfield Yard]
d. **Mitre** Square (Victim: Catherine Eddowes)

If Buck's, Hanbury, Berner and Mitre are used, then in the 1st step the first name "Herbert" can be read in it.

a. Buck's
b. <u>H</u>anbury   H
c. **Ber<u>ner</u>**   er + ber
d. Mi<u>t</u>re   t

Then remains:

a. Buck's
b. -anbury
c. -n-
d. Mi-re

In the 2nd step the family name "Bismarck" can be recognized.

a. **Bu<u>ck's</u>**   B   s   ck
b. -<u>a</u>nbury   a
c. -n-
d. **Mi-<u>r</u>e**   i   m   r

Then remains:

a. -u-
b. -nbury
c. -n-
d. -e

The most meaningful seems to me, if with the "REST" something is to be said at all, NEUN and BURY. The number 9 means so many things in numerology. One can look this up in relevant works or in the Internet. The word "BURY" would be unique in English.

From the street names of the 4 (first) Jack the Ripper victims can therefore result:

Herbert, Bismarck, neun (nine), bury

Herbert von Bismarck (1849 - 1904) is the eldest son of the German Chancellor Otto von Bismarck. He was, among other things, Minister of Foreign Affairs (Minister of State in the Foreign Office) in 1888, and in London from 1882 to 1884.

The question is:
- Was Herbert von Bismarck involved in the murders?
- Was it simply his name that was used/misused?

Buck's Row was renamed Durward Street in 1892. Berner Street is now called Henriques Street.

Herbert von Bismarck's name is easily recognizable. Still, other names should be tried.
If we try other names, only those that do not have the following letters will fit:
D,d; F,f; G,g; J,j; L,l; O,o; P,p; Q,q; V,v; W,w; X,x; Z,z.
Family names like Kramer, Renner, Brenner or Bucher fit, but always the first name of persons known at that time does

not fit. Lothar Bucher (1817-1892) was a close confidant of Otto von Bismarck. Two letters, namely L and O are not in London street names.

Herbert von Bismarck's death in Sept. 1904 coincides with the possible elimination of a confidant in August or September 1904.
There are two other people close to Bismarck who die in August 1904: his father-in-law and a good acquaintance in the Rheingau.

Names of the murdered women - the motive?

   a. Mary Ann **Nichols** born **Walker**
   b. Annie **Chapman** born **Smith**
   c. Elizabeth **Stride** born **Gustafsdotter** (Gustavs-)
   d. Catherine Eddowes (Partner: Conway, Kelly)

Was there a duel in Freiburg im Breisgau in February 1888 in which a grandson of the German Emperor Wilhelm I (1797 - 1888) died? Officially, this grandson died of a lung disease. But friends and acquaintances of Ludwig Wilhelm von Baden (1865 – 1888) knew about this duel. Even they do not reveal the surviving duelist.

I can most likely conclude, based on kinship and speculation as to how insult may have occurred, that the challenger may have been the Scotsman William Douglas-Hamilton, 12th Duke of Hamilton (1845 London - 1895 in Algiers).

That would be ONE motive of perhaps several that I will go into later, but it is the most important one for me at the moment.

a. Ni**chol**s – Walker   H   il   o
b. Cha**pman** – Smith   am   n
c. S**t**ride – Gustafsdotter (Gustav-)   t
d. Eddowes

With these letters I have "Hamilton". I use only the married names until now. In the next step I use only the birth names of the women:

a. N-c-s – W**al**ker   la
b. Ch-p-a- – **S**mith   s
c. S-ride – **Gu**stafs**do**tter (Gustav-)   Doug

From this comes "Douglas", and it remains:

a. N-c-s – W-ker
b. Ch-p-a- – -mith
c. S-ride – -stafs-tter (-stavs-)

It seems that "Eddowes" should be left out because she was the only one never married. Moreover, she was murdered on the same day as Elizabeth Stride.

Then something meaningful must still arise from the rest, because otherwise many other results would be possible.

a. N-c-s – W-ker
b. Ch-p-a- – -mith
c. S-ride – -sta**f**s-tter (-staf**v**-)?

The word "VERSCHWISTERT" (means "siblings") from:

a. N-c-s – **W**-k**er**   w   er
b. **Ch**-p-a- – -mith   ch
c. **S**-r**i**de – -**s**tafs-**tter** (-sta**v**s-)   vers   ist   t

That would cut down on:

a. N-c-s -k-
b. -p-a- – -mith
c. -r-de – -ta-s-

Then there is also "KAISER" in it:

a. N-c-<u>s</u> -<u>k</u>-   K s
b. -p-<u>a</u>- – -m<u>i</u>th   ai
c. -<u>r</u>-d<u>e</u> – -ta-s-   er

Last we still have:

a. N-c-
b. -p– m-th
c. --d – ta-s-

There are 10 letters left, including 1 vowel.
The following words could still be formed:

MAN(T)SCH(T), PAN(T)SCH(T), SCHMAND, CHAMP, DACH, MAHN(ST), MACH(ST), NAHMST, MATSCH, NASCHT and NACHT(S).

Thus, from the married and maiden names of Jack the Ripper's married victims, it could be:

Hamilton-Douglas, verschwistert, Kaiser, nahmst, CPDT.
Or
Hamilton-Douglas, verschwistert, Kaiser, nachts, MPDT.

The questions here are:
- Can anything else be read out?

- Did the duel take place? Was Douglas-Hamilton present?
- Is there a deliberate distraction from other motives?

Total number of letters: 44
Used letters: 40
Letters not used: 04

Further up, 23 letters were used. There would be only 22 if it was "Buk's" and "Bismark".

(du) nahmst	means	(you) took
nachts	means	at night

Traces real or deception?

The reader may form his own opinion on the basis of the many facts whether the traces deposited in 1888 and the events at the death of the presumed principal in 1904 can actually correspond to reality.

Even if the mastermind is recognizable in ciphers or "codes", caution is still required. After all, it could also be a deception to distract from the true causers.

In angles, distances, street names, names of persons and other things like in events months before (motives) and years later (liquidation of a confidant) the executors, the principals and the motive for the murders are recognizable, for Whitechapel yes, for Chicago no.

The book wants to show that for London very much was planned subtly and precisely, in order to find later again the authors - perhaps only alleged authors - of the murders. Does one recognize here the handwriting of intelligent, artistic, high-ranking, honor-impaired and vengeful people? At least it seems so:

While the first motive in 1888 for the London murders seems to come from the Grand Duchy of Baden (Karlsruhe to Freiburg im Breisgau), the second serial killer from Rheinhessen, who only murders in the USA, probably got the order from Stuttgart, for a different motive, also from 1888.

This theory can be disproved at any time if new facts appear.

Crime scenes - calculation (angle)

Leaning Cross - intersection in London

We first have to write down the coordinates of where the bodies were found. This is almost cynical in view of the gruesome events, but it helps us with the reconstruction.

1
Mary Ann Nichols
0.0605° West / 51.52° North

2
Annie Chapman
0.0726° West / 51.5204° North

3
Elizabeth Stride
0.0655° West / 51.5137° North

4
Catherine Eddowes
0.078° West / 51.5138° North

The intersection is then:

As the air line 1 is between coordinates of locations 1 and 4.
As the air line 2 is between coordinates of locations 2 and 3.

The appropriate formula for calculating the coordinates of the intersection is:

$$x_s = \frac{(x_3 - x_2)(x_4 y_1 - x_1 y_4) - (x_4 - x_1)(x_3 y_2 - x_2 y_3)}{(y_3 - y_2)(x_4 - x_1) - (y_4 - y_1)(x_3 - x_2)}$$

$$y_s = \frac{(y_1 - y_4)(x_3 y_2 - x_2 y_3) - (y_2 - y_3)(x_4 y_1 - x_1 y_4)}{(y_3 - y_2)(x_4 - x_1) - (y_4 - y_1)(x_3 - x_2)}$$

From this the intersection point is calculated to:

S
0.0690° West / 51.5170° North

If we do not have 3, but even 4 points, over which we want to calculate the angles between the connecting lines, we must first determine the intersection point. Then we have 4 times 3 points, where the 3rd point is the intersection point in each case.

The intersection point (51°31'01.2"N; 0°04'08.4"W) is found 50 meters north-northwest of the major Whitechapel Road (A11) and 50 meters south-southeast of Old Montague Street.
In addition, it is about 70 meters east-northeast of Osborn Street (B134), which is called Brick Lane further north. To the east, the point is bounded by Greatorex Street. This does not include the smaller streets in between.

Leaning cross-angles in London 93.82°

Annie Chapman
0.0726° West / 51.5204° North

Differences of coordinates in degrees

Between S and 1:
East: 0.0085° / North: 0.0030°

Between S and 2:
East 0.0036° / North 0.0034°

Between 1 and 2:
East 0.0121° / North 0.0004°

The best way is to convert the distances from degrees to meters and kilometers. For this you need the dimensions of the earth.

Earth circumference at the equator = 40075 km,
Earth circumference over the poles = 40008 km.
On average (40075+40008) / 2= 40041.5 km

The distance between two latitudes is then approx.
40041.5 km / 360° = 111.2264 km/°

Latitude/Degree
111.2264

The distance of two longitudes is at the equator:
40075 / 360 = 111.3194 km. Towards the poles it becomes smaller and at the pole (latitude +/- 90°) it is zero.

The distance of the longitudes at a certain latitude is calculated with

$$\cos(Breitengrad) * 111.2264 \ km$$

It is also used 111.325 km, calculated from 40077 km / 360°.

We take the latitude of the intersection because it is a good average, i.e. 51.517 ° north. That makes:

$$\cos(51.517°) * 111.2264 \ km = 0.622282 * 111.2264 = 69.2142 \ km$$

At latitude 51.517 ° the distance between two degrees of longitude is according to the above method:

Length / degree
69.2142

So there is distance between Nichols and Chapman:

$$0.0121° * 69.2142 \ \tfrac{km}{°} = 0.8375 \ km \ (\text{East-West direction})$$
$$0.0004° * 111.2264 \tfrac{km}{°} = 0.0445 \ km \ (\text{North-south direction})$$

And between Nichols and the intersection of all 4 murders:

$$0.0085° * 69.2142 \ \tfrac{km}{°} = 0.5883 \ km \ (\text{East-West direction})$$
$$0.0030° * 111.2264 \tfrac{km}{°} = 0.3337 \ km \ (\text{North-south direction})$$

And between Chapman and the intersection of all 4 murders:

$$0.0036° * 69.2142 \ \tfrac{km}{°} = 0.2492 \ km \ (\text{East-West direction})$$

$$0.0034° * 111.2264\frac{km}{°} = 0.3782 \text{ km (North-south direction)}$$

Distances are then:
Nichols – Chapman

$$\sqrt{0.8375 \text{ km}^2 + 0.0445 \text{ km}^2} = 0.8387 \text{ km}$$

Intersection – Nichols

$$\sqrt{0.5883 \text{ km}^2 + 0.3337 \text{ km}^2} = 0.6764 \text{ km}$$

Intersection – Chapman

$$\sqrt{0.2492 \text{ km}^2 + 0.3782 \text{ km}^2} = 0.4529 \text{ km}$$

In the case of non-right-angled triangles, the unknown angles can be calculated from 3 known sides. With the cosine law:

$$c^2 = a^2 + b^2 - 2ab\cos\gamma$$

Converted according to the angle results in:

$$\cos\gamma = \frac{a^2 + b^2 - c^2}{2ab}$$

or

$$\gamma = \arccos\frac{a^2 + b^2 - c^2}{2ab}$$

$$\gamma = \arccos \frac{0.6764^2 + 0.4529^2 - 0.8387^2}{2 * 0.6764 * 0.4529} = \arccos \frac{-0.0408}{0.6127}$$

$$\gamma = \arccos(-0.0666) = 93.8181°$$

So it results in an angle of 93.82°.

Numerology

First and Last Name of the nobleman 4 & 4 = 8

When I researched the word "Buyen" on the Internet, I was shown among other things that this word results in the number "4" in numerology according to Pythagoras.

1	2	3	4	5	6	7	8	9
a	b	c	d	e	f	g	h	i
j	k	l	m	n	o	p	q	r
s	t	u	v	w	x	y	z	

The procedure for determining the one-digit number that results from a word is the following.

First, according to the system of Pythagoras, we assign a digit to each letter of the alphabet:

Then we take the first name "Herbert".
The digits are: 8+5+9+2+5+9+2 = 40
Then the digits are added from the result: 4+0 = 4
It is added until the number is only one digit.

Now we come to the family name "Bismarck".
The digits are: 2+9+1+4+1+9+3+2 = 31
Then we add the digits from the result: 3+1 = 4

This only works because there is a "C" in "Bismarck". It could also be "Bismark". However, one sees also that it would not work with the father Otto von Bismarck, although "Otto" is a very symmetrical first name.
"Otto" makes 6+2+2+6 = 16, the cross sum gives 1+6 = 7.

Only "nine" (german: neun) results again = 9

In the chapter "Street names - the client?" we had seen that in Buck's, Hanbury, Berner, Mitre via filters after "Herbert" and "Bismarck" still "neun" and "bury" remain.

"BURY" translated into German means, among other things, "to bury, to bury". Because women are killed in Whitechapel etc., and because symbolically the cemeteries in Horrweiler, Gau-Bickelheim and Lonsheim or Bermersheim v.d.Höhe are used for angles and lengths, the assumption is not so far-fetched that the English "bury" is to be read also from the London street names.

Then still the number or digit "nine" remains.
It has a special meaning in numerology because it is the highest single-digit number.

That's not all:
"9" is the only number below "13" where, according to numerology, the number itself comes out again, according to Pythagoras!

NINE = 5+5+3+5 = 18   1+8 = 9 Correct exactly

The other numbers have the following results:

ZERO = 5+3+3 = 14	1+4 = 5	5 too much
ONE = 5+9+5+1 = 20	2+0 = 2	1 too much
TWO = 8+5+5+9 = 27	2+7 = 9	7 too much
THREE = 4+9+5+9 = 27	2+7 = 9	6 too much
FOUR = 4+9+5+9 = 27	2+7 = 9	5 too much
FIVE = 6+3+5+6 = 25	2+5 = 7	2 too many
SIX = 1+5+3+8+1 = 18	1+8 = 9	3 too many
SEVEN= 1+9+5+2+5=27	2+7 = 9	2 too much

EIGHT = 1+3+8+2 = 14 1+4 = 5 3 too few
...
TEN = 8+5+8+5 = 26 2+6 = 8 2 too few
ELF = 5+3+6 = 14 1+4 = 5 6 too few
ZWOELF=8+5+6+5+3+6=33 3+3 = 6 6 too few

What else is added ... coincidence or amazing?

In half of the numbers,
from "1" to "12",
6 times in total,
"9" comes out.

Bury = 3 – the only English word

The English word that sounds like "cemetery" results:

BURY = 2+3+9+7 = 21 2+1 = 3

Angle - like in London – 93.83°

Distance 2 degrees of latitude and longitude

All distances in degrees are best converted into meters. For this you need again the dimensions of the earth.
Earth circumference at the equator = 40075 km,
Earth circumference over the poles = 40008 km.
On the average (40075+40008) / 2= 40041.5 km

The distance between two latitudes is then approx.
40041.5 km / 360° = 111.2264 km/°

Latitude/Degree
111.2264
The distance of two longitudes is at the equator:
40075 / 360 = 111.3194 km. Towards the poles it becomes smaller and at the pole (latitude +/- 90°) it is zero.

Distance of longitudes at certain latitude is calculated with

$$\cos(\text{Latitude}) * 111.2264 \; km$$

It is also used 111.325 km (from 40077 km / 360 °).

The mean latitude of the 3 locations (buildings, cemeteries) in the 3 localities is:
(49.8985° + 49.8509° + 49.8370°) / 3 = 49.8621°

$\cos(49.8621°) * 111.2264 \; km = 0.64463 * 111.2264 =$
$71.6999 \; km$
At latitude 49.8621 ° the distance between two degrees of longitude is according to the above method:
Length / degree
71.6999

Gau-Bickelheim–Horrweiler–Pf.-Schwabenheim

In Germany, the two cemeteries in Horrweiler and Gau-Bickelheim, where the two serial killers come from, and the 1888 house in Pfaffen-Schwabenheim, where the one on the lowest step comes from, fit the London angle of 93.82 degrees.

Gau-Bickelheim /
Cemetery (center) / at main street
Birthplace of Anton Zahn alias Carl Feigenbaum
East 8.0244° / North 49.8342°.

Horrweiler / cemetery (center) southeast
Birthplace of Johann Schmitt alias Joh. Otto Hoch
East 7.9666° / North 49.8966°

Pfaffen-Schwabenh. / Residence built in 1888
Birthplace and residence of Jakob Köth III.
East 7.9478° / North 49.8509°

Differences of the coordinates in degrees:

Between
Gau-Bick. & Horrw.
East 0.0578° / North 0.0624°

Between
Horrw. & Pf.-Schwab.
East 0.0188° / North 0.0457°

Between
Gau-Bick. & Pf.-Schwab.
East 0.0766° / North 0.0167°

Differences of the coordinates in kilometers:

This results in a distance between Gau-Bickelheim (cemetery) and Horrweiler (cemetery) of:

$0.0578° * 71.6999 \frac{km}{°} = 4.144$ km (East-West direction)

$0.0624° * 111.2264 \frac{km}{°} = 6.9405$ km (North-south direction)

This results in a distance between Gau-Bickelheim (cemetery) and Pfaffen-Schwabenheim (1888 house) of:

$0.0766° * 71.6999 \frac{km}{°} = 5.4922$ km (East-West direction)

$0.0167° * 111.2264 \frac{km}{°} = 1.8575$ km (North-south direction)

This results in a distance between Horrweiler (cemetery) and Pfaffen-Schwabenheim (1888 house) of:

$0.0188° * 71.6999 \frac{km}{°} = 1.3480$ km (East-West direction)

$0.0457° * 111.2264 \frac{km}{°} = 5.0830$ km (North-south direction)

Differences between the points in kilometers

Distances are then:
Horrweiler (Cemetery) - Pfaffen-Schwabenhm (1888 House)

$$\sqrt{1.3480 \text{ km}^2 + 5.0830 \text{ km}^2} = 5.2587 \text{ km}$$

Gau-Bickelheim (cemetery) - Pfaffen-Schwabenheim (1888 house)

$$\sqrt{5.4922 \text{ km}^2 + 1.8575 \text{ km}^2} = 5.7978 \text{ km}$$

Gau-Bickelheim (Cemetery) und Horrweiler (Cemetery)

$$\sqrt{4.14425 \text{ km}^2 + 6.9405 \text{ km}^2} = 8.0837 \text{ km}$$

Angle 3 between the points = 93.83°

In the case of non-right-angled triangles, the unknown angles can be calculated from 3 known sides. With the cosine law:

$$c^2 = a^2 + b^2 - 2ab \cos \gamma$$

Converted according to the angle results in:

$$\cos \gamma = \frac{a^2 + b^2 - c^2}{2ab}$$

or

$$\gamma = \arccos \frac{a^2 + b^2 - c^2}{2ab}$$

$$\gamma = \arccos \frac{5.2587^2 + 5.7978^2 - 8.0837^2}{2 * 5.2587 * 5.7978}$$

$$= \arccos \frac{-4.07678}{60.9784}$$

$$\gamma = \arccos(-0.066856) = 93.8334°$$

The bearing over
a) the two cemeteries (center) in Gau-Bickelheim and Horrweiler

seems to be ideal on
b) the angle(s) in London resp. Whitechapel and Spitalfields to fit.

Further point for selection would be instead of the 1888 house possibly the monastery or the cemetery in Pfaffen-Schwabenheim. But at least I would see this house with the year "1888" as a point.

So it results in an angle of 93.83°.

Game with 6 / 60 / 600 Kilometers

Gau-Bickelheim – Pfaffen-Schwabenheim: 6 km

So, after I had seen that the distance from the cemetery in Gau-Bickelheim (or from the center about 150 meters further east at the moat) to the intersection of the (first) four murders of Jack the Ripper in London is exactly 600 kilometers, I had thought on New Year's Day 2021 whether the house of Jakob Köth in Pfaffen-Schwabenheim, built in 1888, could not hit prominent points within Germany at a distance of 6 km or 60 km.

And indeed, that point about 150 meters east of the center of the cemetery in Gau-Bickelheim, which is about the same point that takes 600 km to London, has a distance of 6 kilometers to the 1888 house in Pfaffen-Schwabenheim.

Pfaffen-Schwabenheim – Frankfurt: 60 km

60 kilometers distance from the 1888 house in Pfaffen-Schwabenheim as the air line meets exactly halfway between the cathedral and the Römer in Frankfurt am Main, exactly the middle of the coronation route of German kings and emperors, in the time before 1800.
In Google Maps, measuring the distance (air line), you hit the position of the subway station in the center of the city, that is, near the Schirn Kunsthalle. In 1888, admittedly, this subway did not yet exist; the streetcar in Frankfurt is already in operation at that time.

Pfaffen-Schwabenheim – Koblenz: 60 km

60 kilometers distance from the 1888 house in Pfaffen-Schwabenheim as the air line hits a point about 20 meters before the bridge in Sebastian Bach Street in Koblenz.

In Koblenz on the Rhine (between Mainz and Cologne), it is where the Laubach turns into the Rheinlache (according to Google Maps). This is a very prominent point because the southern end of the Kaiserin-Augusta-Anlagen is located there. Empress Augusta was the wife of Emperor Wilhelm I (+1888). The section from Mozartstraße to this point is also called Swan Pond. Probably among other things in the Internet the Kaiserin-Augusta-Anlage is partly "traded" only up to Mozartstraße. Further north-northeast of it stands since 1896 an Empress Augusta monument. There the "Rheinlache" flows into the Rhine. North of the Koblenz Higher Regional Court and as far as the Deutsches Eck, the promenade is called Konrad-Adenauer-Ufer. The Kaiser-Augusta-Anlagen were laid out by order of the empress from 1856 to 1861. (koblenz-touristik.de)

Therfore this distance to Koblenz seems to be significant as the distance to Frankfurt.

Whitechapel – Gau-Bickelheim: 600 km

The formula for the calculation of the air line is:

$$cos(G) = sin(lat1) * sin(lat2) + cos(lat1) * cos(lat2) \\ * cos(lon2 - lon1)$$

in which
G = great arc
Latitude = latitude = lat
Longitude = Longitude = lon

Gau-Bickelheim, Cemetery (center), at Hauptstraße
Anton Zahn
East 8.0244° / North 49.8342°

London, intersection 4 murders of Jack-the-Ripper
West 0.0690° / North 51.5170°

Pocket calculators use the coordinates in degrees. However, Excel calculates with the radians, i.e. with the factor

$$\text{Coordinate in radians } = \text{Coordinate in degrees } * \frac{\pi}{180°}$$

This results in radians: (in rad)

Gau-Bickelheim, Cemetery (center), at Hauptstraße
East 0.1400522 / North 0.8697709

London, intersection 4 murders of Jack-the-Ripper
East -0.0012043 / North 0.8991413

$$cos(G) = sin(lat1) * sin(lat2) + cos(lat1) * cos(lat2) \\ * cos(lon2 - lon1)$$

$$cos(G) = sin(0.8697709) * sin(0.8991413)$$
$$+ cos(0.8697709) * \cos(0.8991413)$$
$$* \cos(-0.0012043 - 0.1400522)$$

0.7641811*0.7827928+0.64500166*0.6222824*0.9900399

This results in $\qquad cos(G) = 0.9955709$

Now you have to take the arccos of it and multiply it by the radius of the earth.

Middle latitude is:
$$(51.5170° + 49.8342°)/2 = 50.6756°$$

Formula and input options with calculation are offered, for example, on the website "rechneronline.de". At the equator it is 6,378.1 km and at the poles it is 6,356.8 km. The earth is not a perfect sphere.

The mean radius of the earth is: 6365.383 km

$arccos(G) = 0.09415278$

$$\Delta (FH) = 6365.383 * arccos(G) = 599.318 \ km$$

Google Maps = 599.84 km

Using the software Google Maps the distance is

599.835 km

Among other things, this shows that the intersection point in London is about 100 meters north of Altab Ali Park.

Exactly 600 kilometers lie on a water ditch 165 meters east-southeast of the center of the Gau-Bickelheim cemetery.

South of it is a pond, just before the highway A61. North of it flows the Wiesbach, and more ponds are nearby.

Earth simplified as an ideal sphere

Important note: In both cases - either calculation via great circle arc or Google Maps - as also made myself clear in my book "Abt (Abbot) Hadamar bis (to) Rose Hattemer" (2019), the earth is considered as an ideal sphere, which is not true in reality.

But I think, if the exact distance of 600 kilometers was intended by the "constructors" in Germany, which has the appearance, then the ideal sphere was calculated for the sake of simplicity.

This is more pragmatic, because it is easier later for researchers to trace this round distance.

The projectors in 1888 would certainly have been able to determine the actual distance, which is likely to be off by a few 100 meters.

Earth science provides special reference ellipsoids for many points on Earth.

German nobleman in London Code

Even if the person was not involved in the plot - the name was obviously used. To study the vita is worthwhile in any case.

Nikolaus Heinrich Ferdinand Herbert von Bismarck-Schönhausen, from 1865 Count von Bismarck-Schönhausen, from 1898 Prince von Bismarck (*December 28, 1849 in Berlin; † September 18, 1904 in Friedrichsruh near Aumühle) was a German politician.
He was the eldest son of Imperial Chancellor Otto von Bismarck and his wife Johanna von Puttkamer. He participated in the Franco-Prussian War of 1870/1871. As a Seconde-Lieutenant of the 1st Guards Dragoon Regiment, he was wounded at the Battle of Mars-la-Tour.

In 1873 he joined the Foreign Office, where he was at first mainly his father's private secretary, but also served at several legations. Thus he was:
- 1882 embassy counselor in London,
- 1884 in St. Petersburg and The Hague.

In 1885 he was appointed Undersecretary of State and the following year Secretary of State of the Foreign Office.

In the Kingdom of Prussia he became Minister of State in 1888, but his sometimes brusque manner made him quite unpopular with some contemporaries.
He was said to have good prospects of succeeding his father as Reich Chancellor.
When Emperor Wilhelm II asked the Reich Chancellor to resign in 1890, Herbert von Bismarck left office a few days after his father, although Wilhelm had expressly objected to

this. In 1893 he was elected to the Reichstag for the German Reich Party.

Bismarck was a member of the Corps Borussia in Bonn, as well as Wilhelm II. and the brother of the prince Ludwig Wilhelm von Baden (+1888).

In 1881, his affair with the still-married Princess Elisabeth zu Carolath-Beuthen caused a sensation. His father resisted this union with all his might, threatened his son first with disinheritance, then with suicide, and finally succeeded in having the two dissolve their liaison.

In 1892, Herbert von Bismarck married Marguerite Malvine Countess von Hoyos (1871-1945) in Vienna, the daughter of Georg Anton Count von Hoyos (1842 - Aug. 15, 1904) (www.geni.com under Hoyos Family) and Alice, née Whitehead (1851-1936) and thus granddaughter of the inventor Robert Whitehead.
Similar to his younger brother Wilhelm von Bismarck, Herbert von Bismarck died early of a liver disease.
With his wife he had 5 children.

Motive - duel in Freiburg 1888?

Maybe I am wrong with this motive. But it is one of three motives that come to mind for this period around 1888, at least in connection with Herbert von Bismarck. The first is the death of a prince in Freiburg, the second is a suspected insult to Bismarck, and the third the conflict over the colonies between Great Britain and Germany, especially because of Kenya. But I think, the first point fits.

Death at 22, grandson of Kaiser Wilhelm I.

Ludwig Wilhelm von Baden (* June 12, 1865 in Baden-Baden; † February 23, 1888 in Freiburg im Breisgau; full name: Ludwig Wilhelm Karl Friedrich Berthold von Baden) was the younger son of Grand Duke Friedrich I of Baden and Grand Duchess Luise (née Princess of Prussia).
Through his mother, he was a grandson of the German Emperor Wilhelm I of Hohenzollern, who died in Berlin (Altes Palais, Unter den Linden) on March 9, 1888. After studies and military service, the prince joined the 3rd ao. Landtag of the Baden Estates Assembly in its First Chamber in the summer of 1887.

According to official accounts, Prince Ludwig Wilhelm died as a result of pneumonia. There are reports that he was killed in a duel. (Wolf Ernst Hugo Emil Graf von Baudissin: Aus meiner Dienstzeit. Digitalisat (http://www.karlheinz-everts.de/Texte/Dienstzeit.htm))

His last residence was today's Hotel Rheingold in Freiburg im Breisgau. He is buried in the Grand Ducal burial chapel in Karlsruhe.

Officially pneumonia

Wolf Ernst Hugo Emil Graf von Baudissin (1867 - 1926) wrote his article "Aus meiner Dienstzeit" in the "Kieler Neueste Nachrichten" on Wednesday, January 6, 1907.

He wrote:
<< Next May it will be twenty years that I joined the Prussian Army as an avatageur with the 113th Infantry Regiment in Freiburg i.Br.. [...] Freiburg is a pretty town, in the army it is famous because of its scenically wonderfully situated parade ground. [...] How many a snort I got, because the beauty of nature out there interested me much more than the battalion square, which fortunately has disappeared in the meantime.
When there were drills out there on the square, the young Prince Ludwig of Baden, a brother of the present Grand Duke, very often appeared as a spectator. He was a tall, slender, strikingly handsome and seldom amiable person, who at that time might have been barely 25 years old. He lived in Freiburg, listened to some lectures at the university, and since he ate very often with us in the officers' mess, even we midshipmen came into contact with him a lot.
One day he died of pneumonia. Quite suddenly, unexpectedly. Two days ago I had seen him on the street, and when I stood in front of him, he reached out his hand and addressed a few kind words to me.
His death sincerely saddened all of us, we were really shaken.

I stood in the middle of the front of the troops who, at the funeral, cordoned off the road from the small villa that the prince occupied to the cemetery. By chance I was standing in the very vicinity of the house itself. It was evening, as far as I remember, about ten o'clock, and we had to wait a long time until the funeral service was over in there.

At last the coffin was carried out, the rifle was presented, and the funeral roll was beaten on the muffled drums.

Behind the coffin the first to appear was the then already aged Grand Duke, the father of the present one, and there was probably not one even among the crews of the funeral parade who did not have the deepest sympathy with the completely bowed father.

To die so young and so suddenly!

We midshipmen regularly ate together with the officers in the mess hall at noon. Of course, the death of Prince Ludwig was still the exclusive topic of conversation the next day, and even though we were careful not to hear more than we should, we suddenly knew that the prince had not died of natural causes, but had been killed in a duel.

I am sworn not to mention the name of his opponent. But even without this, the whole world knows today who confronted the fun-loving and cheerful prince with the weapon in his hand, in order to demand from him an account for the honor which he robbed from his sister. [...] >>

So much for Baudissin.

"Honor of the sister"

Count Baudissin thus states in his newspaper article in the Kieler Nachrichten in 1907 that the honor of the sister was robbed by Prince Ludwig of Baden.

Indirect witness Graf von Baudissin

Wolf Ernst Hugo Emil Graf von Baudissin, pseudonyms: Freiherr von Schlicht and Graf Günther Rosenhagen, (* January 30, 1867 in Schleswig; † October 4, 1926 in Weimar) was a German writer, journalist and publisher.

The family of the Counts of Baudissin had been resident in Schleswig-Holstein since the Thirty Years' War and produced several military officers and writers. Adelbert Heinrich von Baudissin, the father of Wolf Graf Baudissin, was dike count in Schleswig. In 1871, four years after the birth of his son Wolf, Adalbert Count Baudissin died. His mother, his second wife Louisa Wilhelmine Johanne, was a née del Strother, (* July 28, 1830 Hull/England; † May 11, 1910 in Lübeck).

After schooling at the Gymnasium in Schleswig and the Christianeum in Altona, Wolf Ernst von Baudissin joined the 5th Baden Infantry Regiment No. 113 in Freiburg on May 16, 1887, as a vanguard officer. He received his patent as a Portepeefähnrich on March 22, 1888, after which he continued his military career in Schleswig-Holstein.
When Baudissin retired from the military, he moved to Dresden and, on the advice of his publisher, turned to military satire.
Wolf Ernst von Baudissin died of a sleeping pill overdose in Weimar in 1926, a few months after he had married for the third time.

Swear vengeance on deathbed?

The question is whether emperor Wilhelm I. (1797 - March 1888) assigned his son Friedrich III. (+ June 1888) to avenge the death of his grandson, if it had been a duel at all.

This would fit among other things to the Kaiser-Friedrich-Turm (Tower, built in 1887) in Bingen on the Rhine, which could have been and probably was used symbolically for the 1+8+8+8 kilometers (via Horrweiler and Gau-Bickelheim, where the two serial killers come from, and finally Lonsheim – or maybe Bermersheim v.d. Höhe).

Possible opponent in a possible duel

Track 1: Code in London women's names

From the names of the 3 married women of Jack the Ripper's victims, you can form the following words - if you wish:

Hamilton-Douglas, conspired, emperor, took, CPDT.
Or among others.
Hamilton-Douglas, conspirator, emperor, night, MPDT

Track 2: related to Baden

The Scottish family is related to the family of the Grand Dukes of Baden in the 19th century.

William Hamilton: Too far fetched?

William Alexander Louis Stephen Hamilton, 12th Duke of Hamilton (* 12.3.1845 Connaught Place, London; † 16.5.1895 in Algiers, Algeria) was a Scottish nobleman. He was the son of William Hamilton, 11th Duke of Hamilton and his wife Princess Marie Amalie of Baden. She is an adopted granddaughter of Napoleon Bonaparte. Because of her, King Charles I of Romania is his cousin. The queens Stephanie of Portugal and Karola of Saxony are cousins.

He succeeded his father as the 12th Duke of Hamilton in 1863. In 1864, he was given the title Duc de Châtellerault by the French Emperor Napoleon III. This title had been given to James Hamilton, 2nd Earl of Arran in 1548 and revoked in 1560.

Three years later he faced financial ruin for the first time; but his racehorse winning the Grand National Steeplechase at Aintree saved him. In 1882 he had works of art, paintings and furniture from Hamilton Palace auctioned. The auction at Christie's lasted 17 days and raised 400000 British pounds. The duke was considered coarse and addicted to pleasure.

After the early death of his younger brother Charles George in 1886, he inherited his title Earl of Selkirk.

He married Lady Mary Louise Montagu (1854-1934), daughter of William Montagu, 7th Duke of Manchester, in 1873, with whom he had a daughter, Lady Mary Hamilton (1884-1957), ∞ 1906 James Graham, 6th Duke of Montrose.

Fit for duel over UK school and sport?

Hamilton studied at Eton College and Christ Church, Oxford. There he devoted himself to boxing, horse racing, sailing, and other amusements. He was of stout build, coarse manner, and seemed able to knock down an ox with one blow. He often said what he was thinking.

70

Duels ceased in England in the middle of the 19th century, and in Central Europe only at the beginning of the 20th century.

Sister - reason for possible duel?

The sister of the 12th Duke of Hamilton, Lady Mary Victoria Douglas-Hamilton (*11 Dec. 1850 Hamilton Palace; +14 May 1922 Budapest), was a Scottish noblewoman and great-grandmother of Prince Rainier III of Monaco. She was the daughter of William 11th Duke of Hamilton and his wife Princess Marie Amelie of Baden (+1888).

In her first marriage she was married since 21.9.1869 to Prince Albert, only child and heir of Charles III, Prince of Monaco. The marriage was arranged at the request of the Monegasque princely house. Because Queen Victoria refused a union with one of her close family members, Lady Mary was proposed. The couple had son Louis, who inherited the throne in Monaco.
The marriage was not happy. The princess left Monaco just a few months after the wedding and lived with her family abroad, mostly in Baden-Baden. There she gave birth to her son, who did not see his father until he was 10.
The marriage was dissolved by the church on January 3, 1880, civil only on July 28, 1880 by order of Prince Charles III.

The 2nd marriage on June 2, 1880 was to Hungarian Count Tassilo Festetics of Tolna. The couple had four children.
For 40 years they lived together in Festetics Castle and its large gardens in Keszthely in western Hungary.
On numerous occasions they came together with their brother, the 12th Duke of Hamilton and his great friend, the

Prince of Wales, from 1901 as Edward VII. (1841-1910), King of Great Britain and Ireland.

Older line Baden & Divorce from Monaco

The mother of the siblings a) Lady Mary Victoria and b) William 12th Duke of Hamilton, namely Marie Amelie (1817/18 - 1888) is the daughter of a Grand Duke of Baden, from the older line.

Ludwig Wilhelm von Baden (1865 - 1888) is descended from the younger line of the Grand Dukes of Baden.

We may have a double conflict potential here.

1) Divorce of the sister of the Duke of Hamilton
2) Descent from different lines "Von Baden"

Father – 11. Duke of Hamilton

William Alexander Archibald Hamilton, 11th Duke of Hamilton and 8th Duke of Brandon (*19 February 1811 London; +8 July 1863 Paris) et al. title was a Scottish nobleman and Premier Peer of Scotland.

On February 23, 1842, he married Princess Marie Amelie of Baden, daughter of Grand Duke Charles of Baden and Stéphanie de Beauharnais, adopted daughter of Napoleon I, at Mannheim Castle.
After the marriage, he lived mainly in Paris and Baden (taking very little interest in British affairs).

They had four children:
-William Douglas-Hamilton, 12th Duke of Hamilton (1845-1895)

-Lieutenant Charles George Douglas-Hamilton, 7th Earl of Selkirk (1847-1886), 11th Hussars
-Lady Catherine Elizabeth Hamilton (1849-1894), married the Rev Mark James
-Lady Mary Victoria Hamilton (1850-1922), marries first Albert I, Prince of Monaco, later Prince Tassilo Festetics of Tolna.

Often in Baden and Paris

To note here if necessary: He as a Briton often stays in Paris and in the Grand Duchy of Baden, whatever "Baden" would still be called, perhaps the spa "Baden-Baden".

Second husband of the sister

Count Tasziló Festetics of Tolna (* May 5, 1850, Vienna; + May 4, 1933, Keszthely), prince since 1911, was the son of Count György Festetics of Tolna, who was foreign minister of Hungary from 1867 to 1871, and Countess Eugénia Erdõdy of Monyorókerék and Monoszló.
In 1880 Festetics married Lady Mary Victoria Douglas-Hamilton (* Dec. 11, 1850, Hamilton Palace; +May 14, 1922, Budapest), ex-wife of Prince Albert I of Monaco.

The couple had 4 children:
-Mária Matild Georgina Festetics of Tolna (* May 24, 1881, Baden-Baden, +March 2, 1953, Strobl am Wolfgangsee), married Prince Karl Emil of Fürstenberg.
-György Tasziló József Festetics of Tolna (* September 4, 1882, Baden-Baden, + August 4, 1941, Keszthely); married Countess Marie Franziska von Haugwitz.
-Alexandra Olga Eugénia Festetics of Tolna (* March 1, 1884, Baden-Baden + April 23, 1963, Vienna); in 1st marriage to

Prince Karl of Windisch-Grätz, in 2nd marriage to Prince Erwin zu Hohenlohe-Waldenburg-Schillingsfürst,
-Karola Friderika Mária Festetics of Tolna (* January 17, 1888, Vienna, +January 21, 1951, Strobl); married Baron Oskar Gautsch von Frankenthurn, son of Baron Paul Gautsch von Frankenthurn, Prime Minister of Cisleithania.

On June 21, 1911, Count Tasziló Festetics of Tolna was raised to the rank of Prince by Emperor Franz Joseph, to be addressed as "Serene Highness." He died in Festetics Castle, Keszthely, one day before his 83rd birthday. His grandson Georg (born 1940) is the current head of the house.

Until 1888 in Baden-Baden

The couple thus lived in Baden-Baden from the time of their marriage in 1880 until at least March 1, 1884. At the tragic death of Ludwig Wilhelm von Baden in February 1888, the couple already resided in Vienna.

Mother – Marie Amelie von Baden

Princess Marie Amelie Elisabeth Caroline of Baden (*11.10.1817 or 1818 Karlsruhe; +8. or 17. or 18.10.1888 in Baden-Baden) was the youngest daughter of Charles, Grand Duke of Baden and Stéphanie de Beauharnais. In 1843 she married the Scottish nobleman William Hamilton, Marquess of Douglas and Clydesdale. They become Duke and Duchess of Hamilton after the death of William's father in 1852. Daughter Mary Victoria marries Albert I, the future Prince of Monaco.
Princess Marie Amelie of Baden is a 3rd cousin of Napoleon III of France. At the same time he is her friend as is his wife Eugénie. She often accompanied the imperial couple on

official occasions. She also helped with accommodations when the couple visited.

The family lived at Brodick Castle on the Isle of Arran, and later at Hamilton Palace near the town of Hamilton.

In 1855, she converted to the Roman Catholic faith. After her husband's death in 1863, she returned to her homeland, where she died in Baden-Baden in October 1888.

Death October 1888, Kaspar Hauser

Marie Amelie herself referred to Kaspar Hauser, who was said to have looked like her, as her brother. Her statement gave further impetus to the supporters of the hereditary prince theory. "Kaspar Hauser" was found in Nuremberg on May 26, 1828, when he was about 16 years old. He is said to have been born on April 30, 1812, and died violently in Ansbach on December 17, 1833. "Kaspar Hauser" will not have been another reason for the possible duel in February 1888. Unless it was also a topic of conversation between the 12th Duke of Hamilton and the Prince of Baden.

The Duke's mother died in Baden-Baden on October 17, 1888, at the age of 71. After all, she then died on a "17th" and she was born in "1817". Thus one could form three times 1+7=8. But this will be rather coincidence. Although the death occurs half a month after the 3rd and 4th Jack the Ripper murders on September 30 (Stride, Eddowes). The dates of birth and death are clear on the English Wikipedia, unclear on the German.

Common ancestor of Hamilton and Baden

The family tree shows that the common ancestor of the two hypothetical duelists ("duel" according to Count Baudissin and "opponent" according to my estimation whether code in London) is the first Grand Duke of Baden, namely Karl Friedrich von Baden-Durlach (1728-1811). Although the Briton is 20 years older than his possible opponent Ludwig, the German needs even one generation less.

Karl Friedrich von Baden-Durlach (+1811)
   a) Great-grandfather of Ludwig von Baden (1865–1888)
   b) Great-great-grandfather of William Alex. Hamilton (1845–1895)

Palace Hamilton near Glasgow in Scotland

Hamilton Palace was the stately home of the Dukes of Hamilton until 1919 and was located northeast of Hamilton in the valley of the River Clyde. Here the palace formed the center of an extensive garden complex, the showpiece of which was an avenue extending over five kilometers.
Hamilton Palace was the largest non-royal residence in Britain, and possibly in Europe.
Built in 1695, in the early 19th century the ground began to sink due to mining operations, after which the family was forced to move to Dungavel House, their nearby hunting seat. The castle was demolished in 1921.
To the southeast of Glasgow are the towns of Douglas and Hamilton. After the last male heir Hamilton died out, the title passed to the Douglas.

Bismarck's work with London

1882-84 on site & "à distance" until 1889

From 1882 to 1884, Herbert von Bismarck (1849-1904) was an embassy councilor in London. His political talent was particularly evident in several special missions to London, which he had to carry out as his father's agent in 1882-89.

They concerned, for example, the future of Egypt. In addition, he was to regulate and settle the colonial political tensions that had arisen between England and Germany since 1884.
The agreement on Samoa of 1889 was his achievement.

Character of Herbert von Bismarck

Eberhard von Vietsch's personal description of Herbert von Bismarck (1849-1904) states:
<< Although Bismarck, as a result of his father's backing, had the opportunity from the outset to appear more energetic and outspoken than other German diplomats, he also used his reputation by virtue of his own personality to achieve diplomatic success. However, he always strictly followed the instructions of his father Otto von Bismarck, whose will he subordinated himself to. Obviously, his own will found the highest satisfaction in being absorbed in the service of his father and carrying out his thoughts, but not in independently pursuing his own ideas and intentions. [...]
In view of the generation difference such an uncritical absorption in the paternal will must seem rather unnatural.

It is quite possible that the chancellor's will inwardly shattered that of his son, especially in the struggle over the planned marriage in 1881.

In any case, traits of brusqueness and contempt for mankind appear in Herbert von Bismarck's nature, which betrayed an inner pressure, created many enemies for him and prevented him from a free and positive direction. >>

Revenge for insult?

Undoubtedly, the first and last name of Herbert von Bismarck can be found in the names of the streets of the 4 women murdered by Jack the Ripper (first) in Whitechapel and Spitalfields.

First of all, the question is whether an unknown person wanted to frame Herbert von Bismarck, to associate him with murders in London with which he had absolutely nothing to do.

If he himself was nevertheless involved, the question is what exactly he organized and whether and on whose behalf he had acted.

If he was at the forefront of the murders, then perhaps it could be a personal revenge against British women or men who had offended him. But there is no historical record of that, as far as I know.

Cynical pun

"The cross follows" (>90°) – (Bad) Kreuznach

The question that can be asked is whether the almost 94 degrees in London and Rheinhessen should reference the city of Kreuznach (from 1920: "Bad"). It is not located in Rheinhessen; however, the center of the city is only a few kilometers away from it.

It should be noted that the districts of Planig, Bosenheim and Ippesheim, which have existed since 1969, belonged to Rheinhessen from 1816 to 1969.

Just as "five to twelve" is a common saying, I could indeed imagine a connection here:

"The cross follows!"

Bismarck – "Biß ins Mark" OR "bis ins Mark"

It seems cynically cheeky when the executor of the Jack the Ripper murders bears the surname "Zahn" (Tooth) and the client is "Bismarck" (Bite -or- up to AND Bone marrow).

Both persons I want to see, however, only under reservation in this respective function.

But let's continue to play the game here.

So Anton Zahn bites the 4 women in London in the autumn of 1888 to the marrow in the body. His stabbing with the knife is like a powerful "bite" - in the figurative sense.

Jakob Koeth III. (1850-1904)

Evidence of involvement in murders

Indications for the possible involvement of Jakob Köth III. (1850-1904) from Pfaffen-Schwabenheim (near Bingen, Bad Kreuznach) in the Jack the Ripper murders I had presented in 2015 in my book at that time. These were among others:

- Jakob Köth's death is not registered in the death book of the registry office
- Jakob Köth's death is only noted in the small register book. There the deceased are entered alphabetically.
- Mayor Johann Eibach II (1859-1936) had written "foreign death" in the register.
- The entry is only marked with the year "1904".
- Above it is written Wilhelm Köth IV, died "1904, 08", and below it is written Anna Maria Kraft, died "1904, 09".
- Two serial killers, namely Anton Zahn (1841-1896) alias Carl Feigenbaum from Gau-Bickelheim and Johann Schmitt (1855-1906) alias Otto Hoch from Horrweiler kill in London and in the USA from 1888.
- The geometry of the 1888 house of Jakob Köth III to the surrounding area fits the angle between the 1st & 2nd and between the 3rd & 4th Jack-the-Ripper murders.
- Jakob Köth III may have been eliminated as a confidant after Herbert von Bismarck died on Sept. 18, 1904.
- If there was no direct contact with Bismarck, then the question may arise who a) is otherwise well acquainted with the Bismarcks, b) also dies in the summer of 1904 and c) possibly even lives near Jakob Köth?

Builder 1888 house in Pfaffen-Schwabenheim

The first document indicating the construction of the house in Pfaffen-Schwabenheim is from February 1888.
If one wanted to connect the construction of the house with the presumed duel in Freiburg im Breisgau, then one could compare the date on the documents in northwestern Rheinhessen with the events in southern Baden.
Prince Ludwig Wilhelm of Baden died at the age of 22 on February 23, 1888. The year 1888 was a leap year. This leaves 6 full days left in the month after February 23.

Some questions remain unanswered in case the murders in London are related to the alleged duel at the end of February:
- Was Jakob Köth III still contacted at the end of February?
- Was he involved over the course of the following months?
- When was the angle fixed?
- Was his house construction financed?
- Who and why laid the tracks (names, angles)?

In general, one must ask, who laid what tracks?
I think it is "sporting" if in less than a week after the duel the plan for the murders is so far fixed that there is already a plan for the 1888 house. It looks rather like that street names and angles in London were adapted afterwards to the conditions in Rheinhessen (Rhinehesse). (See in addition with: Variation in Hanbury Street).

By the way I would like to mention:
The exact date of birth of Jakob Köth III in 1850 is in the church register as well as in the registry office. I had the entry shown to me at the registry office in July 2015, but I was more concerned with the 1904 death entry. Therefore, I had not photographed the entry.

Unfortunately, the offices (currently) do not answer e-mails, telephone or partly personal appearance years ago also brings nothing to learn the exact date. However, Köth is also mentioned on the 1870/71 monument, so that his age is thus approximately proven for this book edition.

It can be narrowed down also on the basis of the gravestones on the Pfaffen-Schwabenheimer cemetery.

Jakob Köth II: 23.5.1837 - 10.8.1919

Jakob Köth 4th: 14.4.1864 - 17.3.1924 ("4th", not "IV.")

Johann Eibach records death – his relatives

Johann Eibach II. (1859-1936), mayor 1896-1933, was the cousin of Adam Wetzel (1848-1923), mayor 1886-96.

Eibach's wife's grandfather was Jacob Diegel II. (1805-1891), mayor 1842-49 and member of state parliament 1862-66. Eibach too was member of the state parliament in Darmstadt 1910-11. Eibach and Wetzel were wealthy winemakers. Wetzel went bankrupt in 1899. Diegel was a miller.

Heute Nachmittag 2 Uhr entschlief sanft nach langen in christlicher Geduld ertragenen Leiden unser lieber Gatte, Vater, Gross- und Urgrossvater, Schwiegervater, Schwager und Onkel,

Herr Jacob Diegel II.,

(ehemals Bürgermeister und Landtagsabgeordneter),

im nahern vollendeten 86. Lebensjahre, was wir hiermit tiefbetrübt allen Verwandten, Freunden und Bekannten mit der Bitte um stille Theilnahme ergebenst anzuigen.

Pfaffen-Schwabenheim, den 31. August 1891.

Death notice of Jacob Diegel, who had known August Metz (+1874), the predecessor of Ludwig Bamberger as Member of the Reichstag in Berlin for the constituency Bingen-Alzey (private property), more on that later.

Campaign 1870/71 war memorial

The war memorial was erected by the warriors' association in 1886. From this year until 1896 Adam Wetzel is the mayor. On the plates you can see also the names af Adam Wetzel and Jacob Koeth III., who both had been in France in the war.

Administrator of the village treasury (collector)

Jakob Köth III was also the administrator of the village treasury, i.e. a so-called "collector". After his death, this function passed to my great-grandfather's older brother, Johann Kolb. This great-granduncle, great-grandfather of the present boss of a shoe store in Bad Kreuznach, was the neighbor of my great-grandparents Heinrich Diegel VI and Helena née Wetzel, the daughter of Adam Wetzel and Helena née Diegel.
On a photo of the wedding of my great-grandparents Helena née Wetzel (1882-1941) and Heinrich Diegel IV (1864-1930) in Summer 1903, one recognizes to the right of the groom the couple Margarethe née Diegel (1858-1945) and **Jakob Köth III. (1850-1904).** On the left behind Heinrich Diegel his sister, on the right behind him the brother-in-law Philipp Maus from Bosenheim. Johann Kolb (1863-1943) standing behind Margarethe née Diegel. <u>A picture of Koeth is on page 192</u>.
Opposite the house of Heinrich Diegel, Sprendlinger Strasse 36 "and 34" is the Lutheran church. Today the house is marked "Weingut Sonntag". Johann Kolb lived in No. 32.

Due to the closest relationship it is known to my family that Jakob Köth III. (1850-1904) was the administrator of the village treasury. The proximity is even more true for Johann Kolb. However, the additional occupation "collector" is also written in the address book of 1906 for my great-granduncle Johann Kolb.

By the way, the bride's father Adam Wetzel was not invited to the wedding in 1903 because he had gone bankrupt during the marriage with his second wife, a maid, daughter of a day laborer from Feilbingert. He did not live anymore in Kreuznacher Straße 14. Next to it in 16 was the ancestral home of Kolb. In 18 then Rudershausen lived (barrel with name at the house). Adam Wetzel had to move to a small house in Kreuznacher Straße 78 or 80 around 1900. However, his daughter from his first marriage, my great-grandmother, Helena Diegel née Wetzel (1882-1941) supported her father financially until his death in 1923.

Margarethe Köth née Diegel (1858-1945) had probably disinvited Adam Wetzel from the 1903 celebration. It is certain that according to my grandfather she had negotiated the marriage of his parents-in-law. Her parents house was next to Eibach's house in the Kreuznacher Straße 3. This I did not mention in the german written book.

Did Jakob Köth pay Johann Schmitt alias Otto Hoch from and Anton Zahn alias Carl Feigenbaum through his village treasury? Was money from the mighty in Berlin, Karlsruhe or Stuttgart paid into the village treasury and then passed on to the killers?

Death "abroad" only in the register Aug./Sept. 1904

Here the register with the death entry of Jakob Köth III, which bears the addition "Auswärtiger Sterbefall" (nonresident, external death). Only the year 1904 is clear. The month can possibly be narrowed down to August or September, because the entries above it of Wilhelm Köth IV are on "1904 - 8" and below it of Anna Maria Kraft on "1904 - 9". The exact dates of the other two persons are in the actual death book. Jakob Köth III is not listed there (confirmed by

Mr. Lunkenheimer, until 2015 registrar Verbandsgemeinde Bad Kreuznach).

The cemetery Pfaffen-Schwabenheim has as mentioned the graves of Jakob Köth I., II. and IV. but no grave of Jakob Köth III. His wife (+1945) was buried together with her niece, my great grandmother (+1941). In 1930 Heinrich Diegel IV was buried alone and plain.

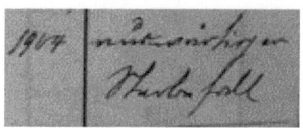

Jacob Koeth's Death only in the Register, not in the more detailed death book. And with the comment: "Foreign death". (Photo from the death register of the Pfaffen-Schwabenheim community)

Wife's suicide March 17, 1945 - US Army invades

The wife of Jakob Köth III. dies of all things on the day on which the US military marches into Pfaffen-Schwabenheim, among other places, on March 17, 1945. My grandfather Karl Kolb II. (1899-1987) reports the death of relatives to the mayor Zöller (also member of the NSDAP) one day later. Two people were killed that day by enemy fire. But not this woman. Perhaps she was one of those who would rather commit suicide than fall into the hands of the Americans.

While some men pull the streetcar out of the village in the direction of Kreuznach, so that the village is not bombed by low-flying planes (soldiers could be in the wagons), my grandfather Karl Kolb II (farmer chairman and 1940/41 as 1st alderman also head of the mayoralty, because mayor Ernst Zöller is in France on war duty) has the barricades of the Volkssturm dismantled in the direction of Sprendlingen. Nearby, Volxheim and Welgesheim put up greater resistance, on orders from above. Bad Kreuznach falls on March 20, and the mayor is shot by the SS.

Margarethe née Diegel (1858-1945), wife of Jakob Köth III., photo taken summer 1903 in Sprendlinger Strasse 36 (private property)

The heirs of the house and the mayors

The builder and the heirs of the 1888 house are:
Jakob Köth III. (1850-1904)
Margarethe Köth née Diegel (1858-1945), his wife
Helena Diegel née Wetzel (1882-1941), great grandmother
Anna Elisabeth Kolb née Diegel (1904-1956), grandmother
Gertrud Zöller née Kolb (born 1931), sister of my mother
And after that my female cousin from Badenheim
See (more) pictures in my german written book.

Mayors (probably) connected with Jacob Köth III.:
Jacob Diegel II. (1805-1891), mayor 1842-1849, in parliament
Adam Wetzel (1848-1923), mayor 1886-1896
Johann Eibach II. (1859-1936), mayor 1896-1933, in parliam.

Jacob Diegel II.   *Adam Wetzel*   *Johann Eibach II.*

The Pictures are copies of the originals. I thank everyone who made the photos available to me: the sister Gertrud Sonntag née Diegel (1907-1989) of my grandmother and the descendants of Wetzel and Eibach.

87

Lots of Köth's in village - wine dealers

In the address book Hessen-Darmstadt from the year 1906, province Rheinhessen, there are very many Köth's in Pfaffen-Schwabenheim. With such a large number of Köth's, Jakob Köth III is only one of many.
Perhaps of interest is the largest villa in the village from this time around the turn of the century 1900. It belonged to one of the 4 wine merchants Köth. After the 2nd World War, I think Stefan Trossen from the Moselle had married into it, who appeared at the wine festivals of the Verbandsgemeinde Bad Kreuznach as a monk of the monastery from the end of the 1970s.
Perhaps the relationship with Herbert von Bismarck or another middleman had come about through a wine merchant Köth.

Niece's relationships with the bishop

The niece of Margarethe Köth née Diegel, Helena Diegel née Wetzel was married to Heinrich Diegel IV. The Bishop of Mainz Georg Maria Kirstein stayed overnight in his house every August 15th (Assumption of Mary) (since 1904). Heinrich Diegel belonged to the Puricelli family's hunting party. (before 1900), according to my grandfather Karl Kolb II. (1899-1987). Helena was given a crosier for her good meal.

Besides:
Heinrich's grandfather's wife was related to the writer and farmer Isaac Maus living in nearby Badenheim. As a trainer, my grandfather won the heavyweight tug-of-war in Cologne in 1926 at the fighting games (Deutsche Kampfspiele).
There are a few more interesting things. Please, see my two books in German.

1+8+8+8 km air line

Lonsheim_Gau-Bickelheim_Horrweiler_Bingen

As the air line from Lonsheim to Bingen has 1+8+8+8 kilometers.

Lonsheim to Gau-Bickelheim: 8 km
Gau-Bickelheim to Horrweiler: 8 km
Horrweiler to Bingen Kaiser-Friedrich-Tower: 8 km
Bingen Kaiser-Fr.-Tower to Klopp Castle: 1 km

The difference of the degrees in north-south direction is the same as in east-west direction
(see the calculation below)!

Namely: 0.18215° +/- 0.00005°.

Using these endpoints:
a) Kaiser-Friedrich-Turm (Tower) in Bingen
b) Center of the Lonsheim cemetery

This is certainly not a coincidence, but constructed or intended in such a way. The question is only, as with all constructions what was caused by whom.

Lonsheim has a Lon(don) in the first three letters.

At singer festivals Pfaffen-Schwabenheim and Lonsheim are represented beside approx. 12 other communities. (tudigit.ulb.tu-darmstadt.de, Rheinhessischer Beobachter, 2.9.1863)

LONsheim is not far from the **DON**nersberg: 21 km. If one wants, one could form the name of the city London from the first 3 letters. 25.5 km is the distance to Pfaffen-Schwabenheim from Donnersberg.

Step 1: Coordinates end points Bingen, Lonsheim

Kaiser-Friedrich-Tower / Rochusberg Bingen
East 7.9006° / North 49.9589°

Lonsheim / Cemetery (center)
East 8.0828° / North 49.7768°

Step 2: Slope of line between endpoints

Slope of the line based on the endpoints is:

$$m = \frac{y_2 - y_1}{x_2 - x_1} = \frac{49.9589 - 49.7768}{7.9006 - 8.0828} = \frac{0.1821}{-0.1822} = -0.99945$$

Step 3: Distance Horrweiler / Gau-Bickelhm. to the line

$$y = m\,(x - x_1) + y_1$$
$$= -0.99945\,(7.9666 - 8.0828) + 49.7768$$
$$= 49.893°$$

You can see here that inserting the X-East coordinate of Horrweiler results in about 49.8966° from the cemetery there. The result is a little bit further south, about 250 meters, in the district of Horrweiler.

Further points for testing (without guarantee):

GB Cemetery

East fixed 8.0244° / North 49.8352°
GB almost cemetery; park, north of the main street, 30 meters north of the entrance of the cemetery

HW Cemetery
East fix 7.9666° / North 49.8929°
HW, 400 meters south of the cemetery, near Aussiedlerhof

Result at fixed east coordinate:

The line Lonsheim-Tower fits ideally to Gau-Bickelheim. In the case of the cemetery even the cemetery is missed by only 30 meters. After all, it is the park opposite the cemetery, also located at the main road to Wallertheim.

Dissolved after X the formula results:

$$x = \frac{(y - y_1)}{m} + x_1 = \frac{(49.8966 - 49.7768)}{-0.99945} + 8.0828$$

$$= 7.9629\,°$$

Further points for testing (without guarantee):

GB Cemetery
North fixed 49.8342° / East 8.0254°.
GB almost cemetery; 60 meters east of center cemetery

HW Cemetery.
North fixed 49.8966° / East 7.9629°
HW 60 meters south from southwest corner of old fortification / 150 meters west from cemetery

Step 4: Distance endpoints east, north in degrees equal (!)

Between
Kaiser-Friedrich-Tower & Lonsheim, cemetery
Diff East: 0.1822°
Diff North: 0.1821°

This is already weird after all the other surprises!

The distances of the angles in east-west direction are the same between the Kaiser-Friedrich-Tower (Bingen) and the cemetery in Lonsheim, namely 0.1821° and 01822° respectively. Someone really played a trick on us.

8.0828° - 7.9006° = 0.1822° and 49.9589° - 49.7768° = 0.1821°.

Step 5: Slope line between end points in kilometers

Multiplied by kilometers per degree it is:

$$m = \frac{0.1821 * 111.2264}{-0.1822 * 71.6999} = \frac{20.2543}{-13.0637} = -1.5504$$

At latitude 49.8621° is the distance between two longitudes using the above method:

Longitude/Degree
71.6999

The distance between two degrees of latitude is approx.
40041.5 km / 360° = 111.2264 km/°

Latitude/Degree
111.2264

Step 6: Distance endpoints in kilometers

This results in a distance between Bingen, Kaiser-Friedrich-Tower and Lonsheim (cemetery) of:

$0.1822° * 71.6999 \frac{km}{°} = 13.0637$ km (East-West direction)

$0.1821° * 111.2264 \frac{km}{°} = 20.2543$ km (North-south direc.)

Step 7: Differences end points in kilometers

This results in a distance between Bingen, Kaiser-Friedrich-Tower and Lonsheim (cemetery) of:

$$\sqrt{13.0637 \text{ km}^2 + 20.2543 \text{ km}^2} = 24.102 \text{ km}$$

Here in this case it is the 8+8+8 = 24 km.

This would correspond to the beginning of the gorge on route 1 from Bermersheim, where the river Nahe works its way to Bingen, in Bingen-Büdesheim. Up to there it is also 24 kilometers.

Only what lies from the Kaiser-Friedrich-Turm on the Rochusberg, Bingen still 1 kilometer further north?
300 meters further NWN: Jewish cemetery Bingen
850 meters further NWN: Klopp Castle in Bingen
900 meters further NWN: Park Klopp Castle
900 meters further NWN:
Masonic Lodge to the Temple of Friendship
1050 meters further NWN: Catholic church St. Martin

Whom Bismarck knows near Koeth

Those who wish can research personalities in Bingen (e.g. Joseph Jonas, steel manufacturer, Lord Mayor of Sheffield), in Alzey (e.g. August Belmont, son-in-law of naval officer, latterly Commodore Matthew Calbraith Perry, who forced Japan to open up trade in 1853) and in Kreuznach (e.g. Anheuser-Busch) themselves.

Wiesbaden:
Paul von Hatzfeldt (b. 1831 Düsseldorf; +1901 London), the German ambassador in London around 1888, took over the Sommerberg estate in Wiesbaden-Frauenstein by inheritance or purchase in 1871/72.

Geisenheim:
Heinrich Eduard von Lade (*1817; +1904 in Geisenheim) was personally acquainted with Kaiser Wilhelm I (+1888) and Otto von Bismarck, as well as son Herbert, because of the Rhine correction and the founding of the viticulture school.

Wiesbaden:
Kuno zu Rantzau (diplomat) (*1843 in Wiesbaden; +1917) was son-in-law of Otto von Bismarck.
One of his brothers was Heinrich Adalbert Graf zu Rantzau (b. 1834 in Hohenhain, Siegener Land; +1891), Prussian lieutenant general. In 1865 he married a woman from Koblenz. Among many other command duties, he was in charge of the 55th Infantry Brigade in Karlsruhe (Baden) from July 10, 1888, until shortly before April 17, 1890, holding the rank of major general from August 2, 1888.

Mittelheim in the Rheingau:
Albrecht von Stosch (*1818 in Koblenz; +1896 in Mittelheim) was a Prussian general of infantry and admiral. From 1872

to 1883 he was first chief of the newly founded Imperial Admiralty. His family originated from Silesia.

He was a friend of the "99-day emperor" Frederick III and, as an old liberal, an opponent of Bismarck's domestic policies.

Rheinstein Castle (Trechtingshausen near Bingen):
Prince George of Prussia (*1826 at Jägerhof Castle near Düsseldorf, +1902 in Berlin) lived for a time at Rheinstein Castle near Bingen and is buried there.

Member of the Reichstag in the electoral district of Bingen-Alzey
Ludwig Bamberger (*1823 Mainz, +1899 Berlin) was a member of the Reichstag from 1874 to 1890 via the constituency of Hesse 8 (Bingen-Alzey). In 1870, he co-founded the Deutsche Bank and was also involved in the establishment of the Reichsbank. In the war of 1870/71, he was an advisor to Otto von Bismarck. However, Bamberger opposed Bismarck's protection policy from the 1880s onward.

First of all, it would be wrong to suspect any or all of the persons just listed here.

Knows Bismarck - near Koeth

Albrecht von Stosch (1818–1896)

Chief of the Imperial Admiralty

Stosch was the owner of a vineyard in Mittelheim. So, like Heinrich Eduard von Lade, this is a relationship with wine, but less pronounced. From 1872 until his death, he was a member of the Prussian House of Lords.

He retired in 1883 at the age of 65. In 1888 he became a member of the Leopoldina (since 1878 in Halle an der Saale). Albrecht von Stosch married Rosalie Ulrich (1822-1902), daughter of the Prussian Privy Councillor of Medicine Dr. med. August Leopold Ulrich and Auguste Hoffmann, in Koblenz in 1845. The marriage produced five children.

Among many other engagements, Stosch fought at Gravelotte, Sedan, Loigny and Poupry, Orléans, and the Siege of Paris in 1870/71, serving as the army's general superintendent.

The number of his national (Hesse, Württemberg and the rest of Germany) and international (Russia, Italy, Belgium, Austria, Spain, Japan, Greece, Turkey, Netherlands) orders and decorations is considerable. It probably amounts to 32 pieces.

The origin of the name Stosch is not clear. So similar sounds "(ver)stosch" in Switzerland for "do you understand".

In January 1872, Stosch was appointed Chief of the Imperial Admiralty with the character of a Minister of State without portfolio. In 1875, he became a general of infantry and an admiral.

Albrecht von Stosch devoted great energy to creating scientific institutes (Seewarte, hydrographic office, and

Naval Academy). In addition, the Imperial Navy was considerably enlarged. The construction of ships was made possible at domestic shipyards. The tight discipline of the Prussian land army was transferred by him to the navy. The latter endeavor, however, often met with resistance from the older naval officers.

Friend of Emperor Frederick III. (+1888)

He was a friend of the "99-day emperor" Frederick III and, as an old liberal, an opponent of Bismarck's domestic policy, which is why he was put up for disposal in 1883 because of disagreements with the statutory pension.

Alfred von Tirpitz, one of his successors

Alfred Peter Friedrich Tirpitz (b. 1849 in Küstrin an der Oder; +1930 in Schäftlarn near Starnberg in Bavaria), from 1900 von Tirpitz, was a German grand admiral, secretary of state of the Reichsmarineamt from 1897 to 1916.
The Reichsmarineamt was an agency in the German Empire (1870-1918), which emerged from the Kaiserliche Admiralität in 1889. Thus, Albrecht von Stosch, the first head of the Imperial Admiralty, is practically one of Alfred von Tirpitz's predecessors.

Heinrich Eduard v. Lade (1817–1904)

Banker, arms dealer, viticulture school

Heinrich Eduard Lade, from 1877 von Lade, from 1901 Freiherr von Lade (also Ladé, * February 24, 1817 in Geisenheim in the Rheingau; † August 7, 1904) was a German banker, arms dealer, gardener, plant breeder as well as amateur astronomer.

Heinrich Eduard Lade was born in Geisenheim on the Rhine in the Palais Ostein, the son of a wealthy wine merchant. He worked as a banker and exporter in Hamburg and Paris.

Through this, as well as through the trade in weapons, he quickly became very wealthy and was able to retire from working life at the age of 44.

Heinrich Eduard von Lade was a man of many interests. In addition to his professional activities, he was very interested in horticulture and viticulture, made a name for himself as an astronomer and was also politically active as a diplomat for the Italian states and the North German Confederation.

In 1861 he built the Villa Monrepos in Geisenheim and surrounded it with extensive parks. The Rosarium alone comprised 800 different varieties with 3000 rose bushes. Here he was also engaged in the breeding and cultivation of fruit and wine. He bred the varieties 'Von Lades Späte Knorpelkirsche', 'Von Lades Späte Mirabelle', 'Grüne Zwetschge von Monrepos' and 'Rote Zwetschge von Monrepos', and the 'Von Lades Butterbirne' was named after him. All these varieties were described in the 'Illustrirten Handbuch der Obstkunde'. For a time, Hermann Goethe was in charge of his pomological gardens.

In 1872, thanks to Eduard von Lade's efforts over many years with the Prussian King Wilhelm I as well as Imperial Chancellor Otto von Bismarck, the Königlich Preußische

Lehranstalt für Obst- und Weinbau, the Research Institute for Horticulture and Viticulture in Geisenheim, which still exists today, was founded by decree.

In 1886, von Lade placed an observatory on the central middle building of the Villa Monrepos, in order to be able to better devote himself to his studies of lunar mapping (selenography) there. The telescope installed there is said to have been of considerable size. In 1897 he arranged the production of a moon globe, which represented on the one side the physical structure of the moon as relief and on the other side the designations of the craters carried. (Note: Lunar maps of the time depicted only the visible side of the Moon). The observatory was severely damaged by bomb hits near the end of World War II and was removed after the war.

In his life, von Lade had to cope with severe strokes of fate again and again. Thus, his wife (1876) and his three children died very early. In 1874, Emperor Wilhelm I visited him in his villa Monrepos and personally inspected the newly founded teaching institution.

In 1877 he was elevated to hereditary Prussian nobility, and in 1901, at the age of 84, he was awarded the title of baron. The town of Geisenheim named him its first honorary citizen on the occasion of his 85th birthday on February 27, 1902. Eduard von Lade died in 1904 in his home town of Geisenheim.

He bequeathed his fortune in the form of a foundation to the teaching and research institute he had established. He is buried in Geisenheim in the family mausoleum in the old cemetery.

The Lade crater on the moon as well as the asteroid 340 Eduarda were named after him.

A monument on the grounds of the Geisenheim Research Institute commemorates the founder of Lade. Another source says that von Lade repeatedly gave fruit to the Emperor (and the Bismarcks). The Frankfurter Allgemeine Zeitung made an article about H.E. von Lade. It says, among other things, that he went to Paris at the age of 18, and then to London. In Hamburg he was successful in a large banking and export business. He became rich as an arms dealer during the US-American war of secession in 1861-65.

In 1854, the Rhine straightening measures begun by the Baden engineer Joh. Gottfried Tulla (1770-1828) were also tackled by a commission for the section of the Rhine between Mainz and Bingen.
The implementation of the measures met with stiff resistance from the Rheingau population. Among others, Heinrich Eduard von Lade from Geisenheim spoke out against the Rhine correction. He was also the spokesman for a petition to the Prussian king and prime minister. This was because Hesse-Nassau had been part of Prussia since 1866.

Contacts with Emperor Wilhelm I and Bismarck:
In contrast to Jakob Köth III, H.E. von Lade had good relations with Kaiser Wilhelm I and Otto von Bismarck.
Whether this is the reason why he is included in the Jack-the-Ripper action is nevertheless questionable.

Whether his name is immortalized somewhere in London? I would only think of the two subway stations Aldgate and Aldgate East, which are located east of Mitre Square, in the direction of Buck's Row. Could mean: "Tag (des) Lade" (german for "day") or "Tag Lade" (english), in german: "Etikett Lade". Besides in english Lade sounds like Lady.

Ludwig Bamberger (1823-1899)

Ludwig Bamberger (*1823 Mainz, +1899 Berlin) was a member of the Reichstag from 1874 to 1890 for the electoral district of Hesse 8 (Bingen-Alzey). Before that, he was responsible for the constituency Hesse 9 (Mainz-Oppenheim) for several years. He took over the mandate from August Metz (+1874), who had known Jacob Diegel II (1805-1891) in Pfaffen-Schwabenheim. Diegel was the Grandfather of Heinrich Diegel IV.; and member of the state parliament Hesse-Darmstadt 1862-66.

In 1870 Bamberger co-founded the Deutsche Bank and was also involved in the founding of the Reichsbank. In the war of 1870/71, he was an advisor to Otto von Bismarck. However, he opposed Bismarck's protective policies from the 1880s onward. He supported the liberal policies of Emperor Frederick III. During one of Bamberger's speeches in the Reichstag in Berlin in 1889, Otto von Bismarck and many deputies left the chamber and let him speak to an (almost) empty house.

In the years around 1888 Ludwig Bamberger was represented in Berlin in a committee "Verkehr mit Wein".

His marriage to Anna née Belmont from Alzey remained childless.

His older brother was Rudolph Bamberger (1821-1900), banker, commercial judge, etc., married to Bertha née Seligmann. He sat for the Progressive Party in the Darmstadt state parliament (Wörrstadt constituency) in 1866-72.

Their son Dr. Michael Franz Bamberger (1855-1926) was in the Darmstadt state parliament for the 1st chamber 1911-18.

His father-in-law Pius Levino (1836-1900) was a wine merchant in Worms and later in Mainz.

Should Ludwig Bamberger propose Jakob Köth III for Frederick III or for Herbert von Bismarck?

Who did the calculations?

Kaiserliche Admiralität

Certainly, the calculations can be done by other organizations or persons, maritime and non-maritime. But after all Albrecht von Stosch lived near Jakob Köth III and was an ex-chief of the Admiralty.

The chiefs of the Imperial Admiralty were:

Albrecht von Stosch (1818-96)
1.1.1872 until 20.3.1883

Leo von Caprivi (1831-99)
20.3.1883 until 5.7.1888

Alexander von Monts (1832-89)
5.7.1888 until 19.1.1889

In the year in question, 1888, Albrecht von Stosch, a friend of Emperor Frederick III who lives in the Rheingau, is already retired.
It is further noticeable that in the middle of the presumed planning of the Jack-the-Ripper murders, i.e. at the beginning of July 1888, the office of leadership is passed on. However, this is different and easily justified. There were differences between Caprivi and the new Kaiser Wilhelm II. Nevertheless, Caprivi becomes Reich Chancellor after Bismarck's resignation in 1890.
Last is a (perhaps trivial) circumstance that the last holder of the post, Alexander von Monts de Mazin, died already in January 1889 during his term.

Leo von Caprivi - as Otto von Bismarck's successor - was Imperial Chancellor from 1890 to 1894. As head of the Imperial Admiralty, he had primarily advanced the torpedo boat business. Because of disagreements with the new Kaiser Wilhelm II, he resigned on July 5, 1888 (Defensive versus competing with England offensively).

But interesting chiefs and their perhaps exciting dates of office aside, let's look here at how the Imperial Admiralty was equipped.

There were the following departments:

- Ministerial Office
- Military Department
- Technical Department (shipbuilding, weapons, etc.)
- Department for budgets and treasury matters
- Hydrographic Office
- Surveying Office

The Hydrographic Office has maritime meteorology and nautical instruments under it. The Surveyor's Office has under it: pilotage, beacons and buoyage, as well as cartography, magnetism, etc.

Kartographisches Amt (military)

The Preußische Landesaufnahme, founded on 1.1.1875, was a subsidiary budget of the Großer Generalstab, which was responsible for the production of topographic map series and the necessary surveying work for the German Empire (except Bavaria).

The results of the topographic survey (coordinates of the trigonometric points, heights of the levelling points, various map series) were used not only for the military, but also for public and private purposes.

Therefore, already in 1875 the Chief of the General Staff and again in 1912 the Chief of the National Survey tried to transfer the tasks to a civilian authority. Each time it failed because of the high costs.

Chiefs of the Great General Staff from 1888 to 1904 were:

Helmuth von Moltke (1800-91)
29.10.1857 to 10.8.1888

Alfred von Waldersee (1832-1904)
8.10.1888 to 2.7.1891

Alfred von Schlieffen (1833-1913)
7.2.1891 until 1.1.1906

Department 3 (of 6) in the Grand General Staff dealt with France and England. Alfred von Waldersee died on March 5, 1904.

1888 Stuttgart – 2. Killer in USA?

Lover Charles Woodcock (bis 1888)

Charles Burger Woodcock (* May 1, 1850 in New York City; † June 26, 1923), who was first named Baron Charles von Woodcock-Savage and later called himself Charles Savage, was the lover of King Charles I of Württemberg, who was 27 years his senior.

Charles Woodcock was born in New York, the son of Jonas Gurnee Woodcock (1822-1908) and Sarah Savage Woodcock (1824-1893). He went abroad to study and found a position as a chamberlain at the court of Württemberg, where he became the favorite of the king, who had previously had several male lovers. In 1888, his favored position with the king and his influence on personnel and political decisions led the political leaders of the Kingdom of Württemberg, especially Minister President Hermann von Mittnacht, to force his departure abroad. Shortly before, the king had appointed him "Baron von Woodcock-Savage". From there he extorted a settlement of 300,000 marks with private and state correspondence, which the king had given him and he had taken with him. In New York he took the surname "Savage".

On June 14, 1894, he married a widow, Henrietta Knebel Staples, who brought 4 sons into the marriage. On June 19, 1897, all of her sons (Joseph, Harry, Herbert, and Leslie Curtis) legally changed their last names to Savage. Leslie Curtis additionally changed his first name to Charles.

Reason for the murders of Johann Hoch?

Are the 300 thousand marks a reason for the murders of Otto Hoch? Is this initiated by Hermann von Mittnacht? A little, but only conditionally, the numerology could help us to see here a connection to the murders of the "Bluebeard of the cattle yard" Johann Schmitt from Horrweiler (Rheinhessen). The air line Bingen - Horrweiler - Gau-Bickelheim - Stuttgart is an important clue.

Woodcock is a bird, in German Waldschnepfe. Literally translated it would be a "Holzschwanz". Matching it with the female names of Otto Hoch, this word would be formed relatively quickly. But this is all awkward:
Schmitz, Hartzfield, Brosett, Tannert, Westphal.
... and looks little like an intention.

Charles Woodcock was 38 years old in 1888

The man was 38 years old in 1888, when he had to leave Germany for the USA, because he was born in 1850.

Numerology: Charles = 3 & Woodcock = 8

Numerologically, the name Charles Woodcock gives rise to 3 and 8.

Let's take the first name "Charles."
The digits are: 3+8+1+9+3+5+1 = 30
Then the digits are added from the result: 3+0 = 3
It is added until the number is only one digit.

Now we come to the family name "Woodcock".
The digits are: 5+6+6+4+3+6+3+2 = 35
Then the digits are added from the result: 3+5 = 8

King Karl I. von Württemberg

Karl Friedrich Alexander von Württemberg (* March 6, 1823 in Stuttgart; † October 6, 1891) was the third king of Württemberg from 1864 to 1891 as Karl. During his reign, Württemberg joined the North German Confederation, which was absorbed into the German Empire in 1871.

Karl was the only son of King Wilhelm I of Württemberg and his third wife Princess Pauline of Württemberg. He studied in Tübingen and Berlin.

On January 18, 1846, he became engaged in Palermo to the 23-year-old Grand Duchess Olga (1822-1892), a daughter of the Russian Tsar Nicholas I and his wife Alexandra Fyodorovna, a sister of the German Emperor Wilhelm I.

Tsarina mother Maria Fyodorovna, the sister of King Frederick of Württemberg, was the grandmother of the bride. On July 13, 1846, the wedding took place in great splendor at Peterhof Palace near St. Petersburg. On September 23, the young couple moved into Stuttgart to the great jubilation of the population.

The marriage remained childless. In 1863, the Crown Princess therefore adopted her niece Wera, a daughter of Grand Duke Constantine of Russia, in her place.

After the death of his father on June 25, 1864, Karl became King of Württemberg and was enthroned on July 12, 1864. Thinking more liberally than his father, he replaced the leading minister Joseph von Linden with Karl von Varnbüler, restored freedom of the press and of association on December 24, 1864, and introduced universal, equal, direct and secret suffrage for the people's deputies in the Second Chamber on March 26, 1868. In terms of foreign policy, Württemberg moved away from alliance with Austria toward alliance with Prussia in the early years of its government.

At the imperial proclamation in Versailles on January 18, 1871, his 25th wedding anniversary (silver wedding anniversary) with Olga, he had himself represented by his cousin August von Württemberg. The king also otherwise showed a tendency to retreat into private life - sometimes outside his country, later sometimes to Nice. In doing so, he neglected the obligations incumbent upon him as a constitutional body - up to 800 unsigned documents are said to have piled up in one case. On the one hand, this was a nuisance for the administration, but on the other hand, it was very convenient for the government, since it could rule largely without interference from the king.

A first "intimate" long-standing "friendship of the heart" with a man connected Karl with his adjutant general, Freiherr Wilhelm von Spitzemberg. Another friend was Richard Jackson from Cincinnati, Secretary of the Consulate of the United States of America. In 1883 Charles met the 30-year-old American Charles Woodcock, a former Congregational preacher and reader to Queen Olga, and his friend, Donald Hendry. Woodcock became the king's new friend. The king also showed himself in public with his friend, wearing the same clothes on joint outings. The king appointed his lover a chamberlain, then Baron Woodcock-Savage, and left him a handsome fortune. It was less the king's homosexuality than the fact that Woodcock took advantage of his position to exert considerable influence on the king's personnel decisions that became a scandal. This did not go unnoticed by the press, and together with the political establishment, headed by Prime Minister Hermann von Mittnacht, the king was put under massive pressure to abandon Woodcock. In 1889, Karl found a new friend in Wilhelm George, the master of machinery at the court theater. This relationship lasted until the king's death two years later.

On October 3, 1891, King Karl returned to Stuttgart from a stay at Bebenhausen Castle, terminally ill, and died here on October 6. A year later, on October 30, 1892, Queen Olga died and was buried next to her husband in the crypt of the Palace Church in the Old Palace.

Prime Minister Mittnacht

Hermann Carl Friedrich von Mittnacht, from 1887 Freiherr von Mittnacht (* March 17, 1825 in Stuttgart; † May 2, 1909 in Friedrichshafen) was a German jurist. He was the first prime minister of the Kingdom of Württemberg.
From 1861 to 1900 Mittnacht was a deputy for the Oberamt Mergentheim in the Second Chamber of the Württemberg Parliament. He was conservative-minded but did not belong to any party.
In 1873, he also became foreign minister, succeeding Baron von Wächter, and in 1876 he became the first minister-president of the Kingdom of Württemberg (official title: president of the state ministry).
Mittnacht - who at the beginning of his political career was rather Greater Germany-minded - always behaved loyally to the German Reich since 1871. However, in the spirit of the royal couple Karl and Olga, he took care to preserve the federal structure of the Reich, especially by holding on to important reserve rights for the Kingdom of Württemberg. Nevertheless, he became a confidant of Bismarck, with whom he did not sever ties even after Bismarck's resignation as Reich Chancellor in 1890.
Mittnacht was a respected authority in the Bundesrat in Berlin. At home in Stuttgart, Mittnacht succeeded in a very pragmatic manner between the politically disinterested King Karl and the Landtag in being the actual strong man of the kingdom during his entire reign, thus putting it on the path of a parliamentary monarchy. In doing so, he based his

policies on the pro-government "Landespartei" and the national-liberal German Party. It is remarkable that he succeeded in doing all this in a predominantly Protestant-Swabian country, although he himself was Catholic and of Franconian descent. In 1854, Herrmann von Mittnacht married Angelika Bucher (1835-1910), the daughter of Franz Xaver Bucher (1798-1859), a member of the Württemberg state parliament. The couple had four children.

In addition to the other honors, two around the year 1888 are of particular interest:

-1887: elevation to hereditary baronetcy

-1889: Knight of the High Order of the Black Eagle

The High Order of the Black Eagle was the highest Prussian order. It was founded by Elector Frederick III of Brandenburg on 17.1.1701, the day before his self-crowning as King of Prussia in Königsberg on 18.1.1701.

By the way it should be mentioned that among others in the year 1888 were prime ministers (from: Wikipedia):

In the Grand Duchy of Baden: Ludwig Turban (the elder)

In the Grand Duchy of Hesse-Darmstadt: Jakob Finger

Jakob Finger (*1825 in Monsheim near Worms, +30.1.1904 in Darmstadt) was married to Marie Millet, the daughter of the Hessian deputy Jakob Millet (*1799 in Paris, +1860 in Darmstadt). Dr. jur. et Dr. med. h.c. Finger, Mennonite, was in the 2nd Chamber of the Landtag from 1862 to 1865. He was professionally active in Ingelheim and for a long time in Alzey.

None of these three men is in any way coded in London. Also with many other politically influential people in e.g. Mainz no name fits the coding in London.

300000 / 30000 / 3000 Reichsmark

Charles Woodcock extorted a settlement of 300000 marks with private and state correspondence that King Charles I had given him and he had taken.

3000 Marks is given to Johann Otto Hoch alias Johann Schmitt during his visit to Germany in 1895.

At least 22365 US dollars Johann Otto Hoch steals from his wives. The question is, to make the idea round, whether it was in truth a total of about 30000 US dollars.

On the other hand, I have not yet been able to locate the exchange rate from German Reichsmark (from 1871) to US dollars during this period.

In 1913 it is about 4.2 Reichsmark per dollar.

Stuttgart – Chicago: 7077 km air line

With Google Maps distance measurement it is 7076 km from the Oberer Schloßgarten in Stuttgart to the coast before Chicago, thus where the Grant Park with the Bukingham Fountain is. The 7077 km is reached with St. Clark Street at the height of the United States Postal Service. Many of the women that Johann Otto Hoch of Horrweiler cheated on or murdered came from Chicago. The distance as the air line to Milwaukee is not less interesting. It is 7003 km to the coast, and 7007 km to Aurora Sinai Medical Center and Marquette University.

Numerologically, one could also get something out of the "7" (seven). The "G" is in the sixth position in "Stuttgart" and "Chicago". The letter is in seventh place in the alphabet.

Maximum variation angle 93,82°

Axis Mitre Square to Buck's Row fixed

Although we have some variation in the Buck's Row-Mitre Square axis, it is relatively small compared to the second axis Hanbury-Berner. This is because Mitre Square is only about 20 meters long and the bearing to Buck's Row (today: Durward Street) runs amazingly close to the course of Buck's Row, i.e. parallel.

In order to be able to depict the first and last name of Herbert von Bismarck on the basis of the street names, the probably German planners could have used Mitre Street, which is at right angles to Mitre Square. This street is relatively short at 130 meters, but still. However, I do not want to carry out a calculation of the Mitre-Buck's variation axis at this point, in order not to complicate the matter unnecessarily. It is enough to play on the second axis, as shown in the following chapter.

Axis Hanbury St. to Berner St. variable

To do this, we determine the westernmost and easternmost points of Hanbury Street and the northernmost and southernmost points of Berner Street (now Henriques St.).

The coordinates of Jack-the-Ripper's first (and perhaps only) murders were:

Mary Ann Nichols
Buck's
West 0.0605° / North 51.52°

Annie Chapman

Hanbury
West 0.0726° / North 51.5204°

Elizabeth Stride
Berner
West 0.0655° / North 51.5137°

Cath. Eddowes
Mitre
West 0.078° / North 51.5138°

In the extreme cases, I would have the following coordinates:

Hanbury max. west point
West 0.0744° / North 51.5203°

Berner max. north point
West 0.0655° / North 51.5148°

Hanbury max. easterly point
West 0.0639° / North 51.5197°

Berner max. north point
West 0.0655° / North 51.5148°

Hanbury St. runs east-west, while Henriques Street (formerly Berner St.) runs north-south.
Henriques Street is approximately 200 meters long. Hanbury Street (before 1888: Browne's Lane) is about 750 meters long as the air line. To get the maximum difference, I have to take the northernmost point of Browne's Street in each case. Because then the axis Hanbury-Berner tilts maximally.

Step 1: Coordinates with west end Hanbury

Mary Ann Nichols
Buck's
West 0.0605° / North 51.52°

west extreme
Hanbury
West 0.0744° / north 51.5203°

northern extreme
Bernese
West 0.0655° / North 51.5148°

Cath. Eddowes
Mitre
West 0.078° / North 51.5138°

Step 2: Intersection west end Hanbury

The appropriate formula to calculate the coordinates of the intersection is:

$$x_s = \frac{(x_3 - x_2)(x_4 y_1 - x_1 y_4) - (x_4 - x_1)(x_3 y_2 - x_2 y_3)}{(y_3 - y_2)(x_4 - x_1) - (y_4 - y_1)(x_3 - x_2)}$$

$$y_s = \frac{(y_1 - y_4)(x_3 y_2 - x_2 y_3) - (y_2 - y_3)(x_4 y_1 - x_1 y_4)}{(y_3 - y_2)(x_4 - x_1) - (y_4 - y_1)(x_3 - x_2)}$$

From this, the intersection is calculated to:

S(W), west end Hanbury
West 0.0690° / North 51.5170°

So it is almost the same as the original points, at least rounded it is the same intersection. Only from the third decimal place it becomes a little different. It is about 130 meters from the west end of Hanbury Street to house number 29.

Step 3: Angle = 105°

Putting all the values into the appropriate formulas, the angle between the west end of Hanbury and Mary Ann Nichols on Buck's Row is 105.44 degrees.

Step 1: Coordinates with east end Hanbury

Mary Ann Nichols
Buck's
West 0.0605° / North 51.52°

East extreme
Hanbury
west 0.0639° / north 51.5197°

northern extreme
Bernese
West 0.0655° / North 51.5148°

Cath. Eddowes
Mitre
West 0.078° / North 51.5138°

Step 2: Intersection East End Hanbury

The appropriate formula to calculate the coordinates of the intersection is:

$$x_s = \frac{(x_3 - x_2)(x_4 y_1 - x_1 y_4) - (x_4 - x_1)(x_3 y_2 - x_2 y_3)}{(y_3 - y_2)(x_4 - x_1) - (y_4 - y_1)(x_3 - x_2)}$$

$$y_s = \frac{(y_1 - y_4)(x_3 y_2 - x_2 y_3) - (y_2 - y_3)(x_4 y_1 - x_1 y_4)}{(y_3 - y_2)(x_4 - x_1) - (y_4 - y_1)(x_3 - x_2)}$$

From this, the intersection is calculated to:

S(W), east end Hanbury
West 0.0642° / North 51.5187°

It is a different intersection point than the original points. It is about 600 meters from the east end of Hanbury Street to house number 29.

Step 3: Angle = 49°

Putting all the values into the appropriate formulas gives an angle between the east end of Hanbury of Mary Ann Nichols on Buck's Row of 48.83 degrees.

Reason for Hanbury number 29 = 1888 House

Three of the four points in London are fixed by the conspirators. Pragmatically, the planners play only with the fourth point, which they can push over the complete Hanbury Street, so that the angle can vary from 49° to 105°. Because of the presumed pun "The cross goes to" (Bad Kreuznach), there remains a margin of 91° to 105°. In the second step - it could look like this - one looks which angle between the new building, the 1888 house in Pfaffen-Schwabenheim and the two cemeteries in Horrweiler and Gau-Bickelheim results. This calculates to approx. 93.83° +/- 0.01° (calculation of the author). Then one puts this angle on

London and finds out that with it the house in the Hanbury St. No. 29 is hit.

In other words:

If the acreage or building land of Jakob Köth III. (1850-1904) had been one or two plots further west towards Bosenheim and Bad Kreuznach or one or two plots further east towards Sprendlingen in Rheinhessen, then a different angle would have been used in London and thus a slightly different house number in Hanbury Street, e.g. 25 or 33.

Perhaps one takes also therefore this Mr. Köth (there are many other Köth in Pfaffen-Schwabenheim), because he wants to build straight a house.

As already written in another place:

On the other hand, the Köth have e.g. in the address book of 1906 four wine merchants to show. There is only one Mr. Hörbrand as wine merchant in the village. In some villages of Rheinhessen there are no persons at all in this profession, e.g. in Horrweiler or Lonsheim. Although Jakob Köth III is not a wine merchant, his relatives are. In addition, he administers the village treasury.

So you can only "play" on Hanbury Street because:
- Buck's Row and Berner Street run parallel,
- Mitre Square and Mitre Street are too short,
- Hanbury Street is perpendicular to the connection between two crime scenes, of which the cross is.

Planning in London

Selection of the storage locations for the corpses

First, the German side obtains a map of Whitechapel and Spitalfields in London, which is obvious, preferably with a street directory.

Then the streets were obviously selected on the basis of the first and last name of Herbert von Bismarck. There the 4 women - murdered - should be deposited. In the first case at least, with Mary Ann Nichols, the place of the murder does not agree with the place where the body was deposited. The London police had found this out. The decisive factor is the place of deposit, which was deliberately chosen by the German conspirators.

Another task of the planning is that the angle between the 4 places of deposit of the corpses in London must fit exactly to the triangle in Rheinhessen.

Selection of women based on their names

The first 3 victims of Jack the Ripper were married. The fourth victim was not. Moreover, the 4th victim was murdered on the same day as the 3rd victim. Only Annie Chapman on Hanbury Street is not murdered at the end of the month. Both of these items are certainly meant to say something.

The birth names and the last names of the husbands of these 3 women Mary Ann Nichols, Annie Chapman and Elizabeth Stride point to the motive of the murders.

Because in the names of the women we read the conspiracy with the German Emperor Wilhelm I (+1888) and the name of a Scottish nobleman, who had possibly killed the Baden grandson of the Emperor in a presumed duel in Freiburg im Breisgau, in February 1888.

Here the question is, which of the German conspirators (essentially Prussia, Baden and Hesse-Darmstadt) is able to find from a large number of prostitutes in Whitechapel and Spitalfields exactly those, who can depict the name of the Scottish nobleman William Douglas-Hamilton.

It must have been precisely researched here on foreign territory (England), and within a few months (March to August 1888).
I think that Jakob Köth III in Pfaffen-Schwabenheim did not have the possibilities at least for this partial task, hard to imagine. How does the perhaps Prussian or Baden secret service proceed here? Does one ask on the spot in Spitalfields in spring 1888? Or does one have an informer at a London authority obtain the lists of prostitutes?

Selection of killers for London and USA

Had Köth chosen the two killers Anton Zahn and Johann Schmitt or did someone else do it for him? Was Köth only supposed to introduce the two murderers? It is hard to imagine that Köth had nothing to do with the matter at all. So, that the Prussian secret service (or that of Hesse-Darmstadt) simply used his house as a coordinate and he didn't know anything about it. Because why else would he (presumably) have been taken out of the way in 1904?

Interesting are then the two men from Gau-Bickelheim and Horrweiler: Clearly, the two villages were chosen on the one hand because of the angle on Pfaffen-Schwabenheim and on the other hand because of the 1+8+8+8 kilometer distance between Bingen and Lonsheim (possibly Bermersheim vor der Höhe) near Alzey.

Here the question forces itself with a slightly indignant laughter whether not in every locality of Rheinhessen or elsewhere in Germany always a man can be found who (if necessary against good payment by the secret service) secretly kills women (or men) in large numbers.

Calculation of 1+8+8+8 km, who?

In another chapter we see that the 1+8+8+8 km distance fits ideally to Lonsheim, where at that time still a Mrs. Barth née Köth lived. Moreover, the difference of the coordinates between Bingen and Lonsheim in north-south direction is the same as in east-west direction. This would not be the case with Bermersheim. Because of "Köth" in Lonsheim, "1+8+8+8 km" may have been mathematically calculated by Jakob Köth III. But because of the bearing to Stuttgart, which fits ideally, this is perhaps beyond his possibilities.

Choice of days for the murders

It is each of the weekends (August 31, September 8 and 30). It is twice the last day of the month.

The order of the murders, and that the first two murders are one week apart, should give some information about which of the two possible angles in an oblique cross is meant.

If I do not cross two air lines with exactly 90 degrees (or zero degrees), then I have two equal angles twice. This is the nature of continuous straight lines or lines. Two equal angles α are related to the other two equal angles β by a ratio of 180 degrees minus α or β.

This means that if I know a single one of the 4 angles, then the other 3 angles are clearly fixed.

These angles are counterclockwise:

1) Murder 1 and Murder 2 = 93.82° (+/- 0.01°).
2) Murder 2 and Murder 4 = 180° - 93.82° = 86.18°
3) Murder 4 and Murder 3 = 93.82°.
4) Murder 3 and Murder 1 = 86.18°.

So, from the order of the murders, it can be seen that the nose of the detective investigating these murders should be pressed to the angle 93.82° (And not to the angle 86.18°).
After all, the angle between Pfaffen-Schwabenheim, Horrweiler and Gau-Bickelheim has 93.83° (+/- 0.01°) and the nearby city of Bad Kreuznach on the Nahe has the designation "Kreuz-nach", so the cross does not go "BEFORE" (less 90°) but "AFTER" (greater 90°).

Site inspection in London

So that Anton Zahn alias Carl Feigenbaum (1841-1896) places the 4 women presumably killed by him correctly according to the specification of the obviously German organizers, he would have had to have been in London before. This happened then with security before August 31, 1888, and in company with German introducer.

Both persons must have walked e.g. in July 1888 the 4 places, Bucks Row, Hanbury Street, Berner Street and Mitre Square, in such a way that Anton Zahn from Gau-Bickelheim finds these places also at night ("in sleep"). Perhaps this happened several times, for practice....

If Anton Zahn (as happened with Mary Ann Nichols) does not kill the women at the same place where they were found later, then he may have to get the lifeless body(s) there over hundreds of meters at night. The question is whether a second person did not always help with the murders, even if it was with a horse-drawn carriage or a hand-drawn cart. Perhaps this second person also functioned as a warner so that the murders would not be disturbed by random third parties passing by.

It is a completely different challenge for Anton Zahn to find the selected women on exactly those nights that were planned. Not only must the 4 women Nichols to Eddowes have been selected by the secret service beforehand - no - Anton Zahn must also be introduced to exactly these 4 women. Does he get acquainted with the women days or weeks before? Does a second man guarantee their availability?

It is true that Anton Zahn must be the last in the chain to make contact with the women. But he needs one or more people to help him a) to get exactly these women b) at the right time c) at the right place "in front of the shotgun" for him. He arranged to meet Catherine Eddowes shortly before the murder of Elizabeth Stride. Here we know what Anton Zahn's part in the action was. The Eddowes, however, unlike the first 3 women Nichols, Chapman and Stride, was arbitrarily interchangeable. She may have just had to be unmarried. Anton Zahn could have managed that on his own under certain circumstances.
With the other 3 women he must have been supported in any case, and massively.

In the case of Elizabeth Stride, the London police recorded that the murderer was disturbed and almost caught, by Mr.

Diemschutz. Did another German person "stand lookout" here and warn the killer? Stride even refused one of the "suitors" that evening.

City map London 1888 and murders

In this map, created by a London authority, 2 murders are marked before the 4 Jack-the-Ripper murders and 1 murder after. A 5th Jack-the-Ripper, the one on Mary Jane Kelly, belongs to another murderer in my opinion. It may have been added on purpose and declared canonical because it makes the cross not too visible anymore that results from the first four murders. In addition, the drawing in of two older murders, of the women Tabram and Smith, is also confusing. This is one of the few city maps that is in the public domain. The downside, however, is that the location of the 2nd Jack-the-Ripper murder is drawn incorrectly. Hanbury Street house number 29 is one block further east than drawn, there about centered. Some city maps with the canonical 5 Jack-the-Ripper murders are correct.

I had worked with this incorrect drawing in 2015 and had come up with an angle of about 95 degrees by drawing, but it is not correct. With knowledge of the exact positions of the murders one comes to an angle of 93.82°.

By chance I had determined in 2015 an angle of 93.23° between Horrweiler, Gau-Bickelheim and Pfaffen-Schwabenheim, because I wanted to get equal distances from the third place to the other two. However, I had not used the cemeteries in 2015, but the old restaurant in Horrweiler (there is no town hall in Horrweiler) and the town hall in Gau-Bickelheim.

(Map with 7 red spots is used in Wikipedia, file is called: "Whitechapel Spitalfields 7 murders.PNG")

Family of Anton Zahn 1789 to 1840

Grandparents, aunts, uncles, bases, cousins

Little is known about the siblings of Anton Zahn's (1841 - 1896) mother Catharina née Zahn from Eckelsheim near Wöllstein. She probably has a half-sister Maria Anna Zahn, who is baptized on 17.2.1797.

The grandparents on the mother's side are Valentin Zahn (May 1774 - May 1, 1845) and Maria Carolina née Welzing (born 1779 in Volxheim). The parents of the mother Catharina (1801 - 1876) marry on March 11, 1798 in Wöllstein. Valentin Zahn dies in Gau-Bickelheim.

The peasant upper class (here: Rheinhessen) marries the mostly more distant relatives (e.g. 3rd cousins) for generations, even across more distant localities (10 or 20 kilometers).

For a Carl Zahn from Eckelsheim also married to Gau-Bickelheim around 1800 and died there around 1850. Some of the parents of Valentin Zahn again come from Gau-Bickelheim.

Already fully documented is the kinship of the father Anton Zahn senior (1800 - 1855). Anton Zahn junior also gets to know the second grandfather a little bit at a very young age. The grandparents on the father's side are Jacob Zahn (May 9, 1765 - June 13, 1844) and Anna Maria née Haas (Oct. 28, 1768 - Jan. 23, 1838). Both were born and died in Gau-Bickelheim.

Jack the Ripper candidate Anton Zahn thus experienced the deaths of both his grandfathers at the ages of three and four. He did not live to see at least one grandmother.

The question here is whether the grandfathers can have any influence at such a young age. Precisely because the grandmothers are missing.

Another point would be whether the little boy feels more secure with the men than with the women.

In addition to the grandfathers, there remain the parents, the aunts and uncles, and initially only the five older brothers. There are also the cousins and bases (cousins).

The weight is clearly on the male side, at least in the immediate environment.

Female elements come only from the mother. Then only from the aunts, especially the father's older sister, and their daughters, Anton's cousins, who are a generation older.

The paternal grandparents have the following children:
- Catharina Helena (get. 19 Nov. 1789, + 17 Dec. 1869).
- Anna Margaretha (get. 26. July 1791)
- Maria Fides (d. Nov. 26, 1792)
- Mathias (baptized Dec. 2, 1794)
- Catharina (d. Nov. 1, 1796)
- Valentin (d. Dec. 15, 1798, buried April 2, 1806)
- Anton (get. 13. April 1800, + 5. Nov. 1855)
- Johann (get. Jan. 19, 1802, buried April 19, 1810)
- Anna Maria (get. Jan. 21, 1804, + before 1810)
- Jacob (get. Dec. 20, 1805)
- Catharina Franziska (get. 17. Aug. 1808, marriage 1839)
- Anna Maria (get. Feb. 19, 1810, marriage 1837)
- Martin (get. Nov. 11, 1812)

If the four children born between 1791 and 1796 had also died prematurely, then the eldest daughter Catharina Helena would be followed by Anton Zahn's father Anton.

The author of this book also has ancestors in Gau-Bickelheim via the Gau-Algesheim Hattemer. Jakob Weis (ancestor no. 66) (*17 Feb. 1761 in Gau-Bickelheim) marries Katharina née Daum (ancestor no. 67) (*5 April 1759 in Badenheim) on 11 Jan. 1782 in Gau-Algesheim. Benedikt Weis (ancestor no.

132) was born in Gau-Bickelheim and married Maria Elisabeth née Bornheimer (ancestor no. 133) there in 1754.

Conflict aunt, father

In the following chapters, it will be shown that there could have been a rift between Anton Zahn's father and his older sister. The maximum of this hypothetical conflict probably falls exactly in the years 1840 and 1841, when Anton Zahn was conceived and born.

First of all, the author would like to point out that there were great upheavals in the world politics when the elder sister was born in 1789 (the beginning of the French Revolution) and the brother in 1800 (during this period: Napoleon Bonaparte's assumption of power).

The aunt Catharina Helena née Zahn married a Franz Becker in 1811.

After Catharina Helena Becker née Zahn gave birth to several children between 1811 and 1823, her husband Franz Becker supposedly died around 1823.

Apparently, Anton Zahn's aunt was now on her own with the children from 1822 or 1823.

Two cousins weddings 1840

The three successive events
- Marriage of the two cousins in 1840,
- the rejected emigration of the parents in 1840 and the
- birth in 1841 of Anton Zahn
belong together.

They are important for the special situation of Anton Zahn. Even if these three points are by no means all.

After two younger sisters of the father Anton Zahn senior (1800 - 1855) had married in 1837 and 1839, it was already the turn of two nieces of the father with a double marriage in the middle of 1840.

First, the cousin (base) of Anton Zahn, who was not even conceived at that time, Anna Maria née Becker (baptized 31 October 1817) married Heinrich Weigand (born 1814) on 30 June 1840 in the old church (torn down in 1842 because of dilapidation) in the village center of Gau-Bickelheim.

Heinrich Weigand is "civis et sociniärius" and illegitimate son ("filius illegit.") of Anna Margaretha Weigand from Schimsheim.

The bride is the daughter of (deceased?) "civis et agricol." (citizen and farmer) Franz Becker and Catharina Magdalena née Zahn.

Two weeks later, on July 12, 1840, the sister Catharina born Becker (born and baptized on August 31, 1819) marries Michael Joh. Pfeiler (35 years and 7 months old), "civis, qui pictines fabricatur in Alzey" (citizen, craftsman, more precisely painter or varnisher in Alzey). The age of Catharina née Becker is recorded by the Catholic priest in the church book as 21 years and three months. Strictly speaking, it is 21 years minus 1.5 months. Only the parents of the bride are noted.

The mother is given as "Catharina Magdalena" and not as "Catharina Helena". Whether the bride's father Franz Becker is already deceased, as it is entered in familysearch.org ("+ before 1823"), cannot be seen in the many small abbreviations.

Discarded emigration 1840

The private researcher who looks at the documents and books of the offices and authorities of Hesse-Darmstadt in the 19th century under the website arcinsys.de (successor of hadis.hessen.de) will be astonished to find under the keyword "emigration" in Rheinhessen between 1830 and 1860 that especially in Gau-Bickelheim there were extremely many emigrations or more precisely "officially noted wishes to emigrate".

Not everyone who had himself written down by the authorities actually left Germany. Conversely, there are people who turned their backs on their homeland but did not have themselves noted down. Thus, the quantities should be about right as far as the number of emigrants is concerned, if one considers only those who were noted.

Gau-Bickelheim had according to the website alemania-judaica.de

- In 1819   31 Jews, 1311 Catholics and 17 Protestants.
- In 1865   43 Jews, 1282 Catholics and 12 Protestants.
- In 1905   28 Jews, 1196 Catholics and 36 Protestants.

As was the case in the Rheinhessen patchwork, neighboring communities could be extremely Protestant (either radical Calvinist or moderate Lutheran) or extremely Catholic.

There were also places in Rheinhessen where the proportion of Catholics and Protestants was balanced. The only church in the village or small town was usually used by both denominations.

Only around 1900, in the course of general prosperity, a second church was added.

Now for Pfaffen-Schwabenheim, for example, between 1840 and 1850 there is no wish to emigrate at all in the notes of the Alzey, Mainz or Darmstadt authorities. It looks the same with the neighboring Badenheim, the residence of the peasant poet and Protestant farmer Isaak Maus. In 1858 two emigrants are found in Pfaffen-Schwabenheim for the USA: Georg Kolb, 41 or 47 years as, farmer and Bertram Marcy.

In Wallertheim (Verbandsgemeinde Wörrstadt), east of Gau-Bickelheim six families are noted between 1840 and 1850 to emigrate to the USA: Huf, Jöckel (2x), Schowalter, Schreyer and Barth.

Here at this point it should be mentioned that Gau-Bickelheim belonged to the Electorate of Mainz until 1792 (due to the fact that it belonged to the Amt Gau-Algesheim am Rhein).

Between 1792 and 1798 (time of the French conquests and "Teutonic" reconquests) the village was then assigned to Wöllstein. Thus the village again lies in a peripheral position of an administrative unit. Wöllstein is not to be confused with Wörrstadt.

In the somewhat larger Sprendlingen (Rheinhessen) about 10 emigrants are issued between 1840 and 1850. In Gau-Algesheim on the Rhine there are about 20 families. In Armsheim there are about 15 families in the period 1850 to 1860. Even the larger village of Wöllstein does not have such a high emigration rate as Gau-Bickelheim.

In Gau-Bickelheim there is a true emigration rage.

Caused by probably strong child wealth, by perhaps bad harvests, housing shortage, speculative scaremongering of the local church or the mayor. The reasons may be manifold. We have the following emigrations or desires in Gau-Bickelheim:

- Emigration destination Algeria, Date April 1844, families or individuals Beck, Rösch, Jahn, Wolff, Sutter, Schuhmacher, Fuhr, Krollmann (2x), Weitzel, Gezberg.
- Emigration destination USA, Date April 1840 bis 1846, families or individuals Bork, Arnold, Michel, Fuhr, Schmitt, Beck, Hönig, Bornheimer, Frohndorf, Scheppler, Maus, Weis.

- Emigration destination USA, Date 1854 bis 1859, families or individuals Hahn, Boos, Klein, Faßbinder.
- Emigration destination West indies, Date Jan. & Febr. 1840, families or individuals Bork, Joseph Wolf, Susanna Wolf born Weis with destination British Guyana.
- Emigration destination Brazil, Date March 1858, families or individuals Frosch, Jacob Strohband (57 years old), Bornheimer, König, Schröder, Weitzel, Seelig, Krollmann.
- Emigration destination Brazil, Date Febr. 1859, families or individuals Haas, Freiland, Mathias Zahn II. (Craftsman, years old) with his wife Anna Marg. born Hammer (38 years old) and six children aged between six and thirteen.
- Emigration destination Australia, Date Febr. 1840, families or individuals Jacob Weitzel (Manual worker, 34 years old) with his wife Catharina born Sotang (34 years old).
- Emigration destination Australia, Date April 1840, families or individuals Johann Friedrich (farmer, 44 years old) with his wife Elisabet born Dreibus (51 years old), Anton Zahn (farmer, 40 years old) with his wife Catharina née Zahn (39 years old) and the five children Jacob (14 years old) , Carl (12 years old), Johann (9 years old, appeared before the press in New York in 1896 after the execution of his brother Anton), Martin (6 years old), Mathias (2 years old, married in 1866 to Hofheim near Bensheim).

As can also be seen here, the daughter or sister Anna Margaretha (b. 1830, d. 1832) is no longer alive in 1840. Anton Zahn (1841 - 1896) is right in a certain sense when he claims in Sing Sing prison in New York to have two sisters. However, it also becomes clear why he only inherits the sister Magdalena (b. 1847). His brothers are left empty-handed in the will.

Among the emigrants from Gau-Bickelheim there are still two young men who avoid the military service of Hesse-Darmstadt. In 1852, they submit a request to emigrate "overseas". Franz Hammer and Jacob Fuhr have the remark: "Avoiding the military service obligation".

By the way, from Zotzenheim (between Gensingen and Sprendlingen and thus between Horrweiler and Gau-Bickelheim) migrates in November 1855 a Johann Ramb II. (day laborer, 46 years) emigrated with his wife to "America, South", e.g. to Argentina. The family name Ramb, which also exists in Horrweiler, becomes interesting in connection with the serial killer Johann Schmitt (1855 - 1906) alias Johann Otto Hoch. He immigrates to the USA in 1888, of all years, after leaving his wife, a née Ramb, in 1887.

The emigration of Anton Zahn senior (1800 - 1855) and his family to Australia (recorded by the authorities in April 1840) does not take place.

It almost looks as if the two weddings of his nieces in June and July 1840 were only performed because Anton had promised his older sister Catharina to emigrate.

Right now Anton's (1800 - 1855) wife Catharina (1801 - 1876) is pregnant with Jack the Ripper candidate Anton junior (1841 - 1896).

It would not be surprising if the little boy would feel all the hatred of the relatives from his father's sister, especially from his much older cousins (bases), one of which is proven to have been born on August 31.

But this insinuation of the author cannot be proved. Indications from 1863 to 1888 are listed in the following, which are much more valid.

It is also possible that other women and men inflicted mental perversions on little Anton Zahn. In this context, the two-year stay of his older brother Carl (b. 1828) from 1846 to 1848, when Anton was just five to seven years old, is particularly striking.

Only one thing is fairly certain. Usually a person gets a mental crack in his early childhood, when he can't explain the disturbance as an adult, or can't get it out of his subconscious, despite his understanding. In the case of Anton Zahn there must have been something like that. Otherwise, his behavior in 1894 and his statements from 1894 to 1896 in the USA cannot be explained.

Zur Erinnerung an die glorreichen Siege der deutschen Armee gegen Frankreich 1870-71, monument in Pfaffen-Schwabenheim

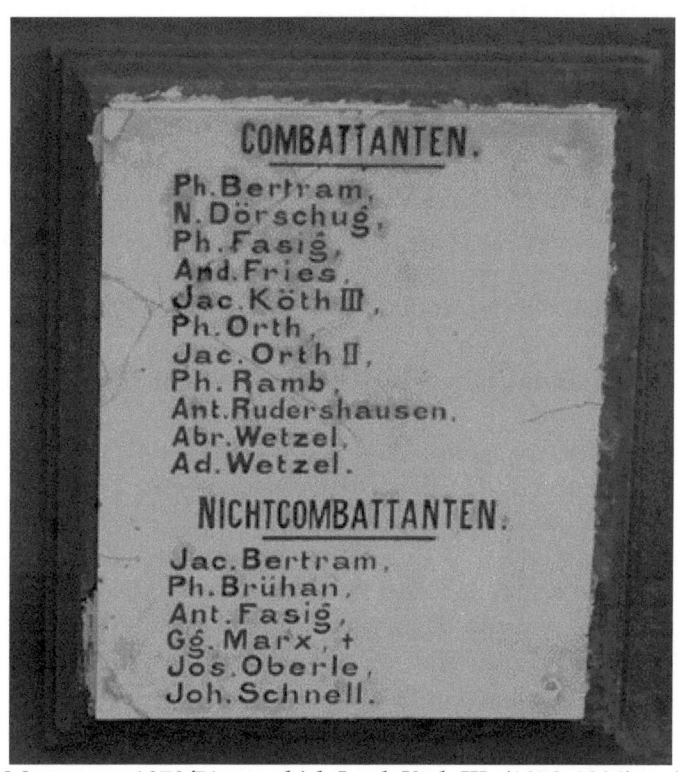

COMBATTANTEN.

Ph. Bertram,
N. Dörschug,
Ph. Fasig,
And. Fries,
Jac. Köth III,
Ph. Orth,
Jac. Orth II,
Ph. Ramb,
Ant. Rudershausen,
Abr. Wetzel,
Ad. Wetzel.

NICHTCOMBATTANTEN.

Jac. Bertram,
Ph. Brühan,
Ant. Fasig,
Gg. Marx, †
Jos. Oberle,
Joh. Schnell.

Monument 1870/71, on which Jacob Köth III. (1850-1904) and
Adam Wetzel (1848-1923) are mentioned (private)

133

Anton Zahn – Childhood

Birth 1841 in Gau-Bickelheim

According to the Catholic church register Anton Zahn was born on May 17, 1841 and baptized on the same day by priest Norbert Körber (in office 1836 - 1848). The parents are Anton Zahn "civis et mercenarius" and Catharina Zahn née Zahn. His godparents are Antonia Zahn and Mathias Zahn.

Church demolished in 1842 and rebuilt 1853

In 1842, one year after Anton Zahn's birth, the old church on the village square in the center was demolished because it was in danger of collapsing.
Possibly this is a drastic experience for Anton Zahn.
The construction of a new church on the southern edge of the village, directly on the country road from Wöllstein via Gau-Bickelheim to Wallertheim and on to Nierstein on the Rhine, cannot begin until 1845.
The construction work continues until the consecration in 1853.
Until then, the parish probably only had a baroque parish hall for masses and sacraments. (However, the author has not verified the parish hall and it is speculation).
The tower that is visible today was added only in 1929/1930.

Lightning strikes this new church in the 1880s. The wall paintings have to be renewed at that time.

Condemnation of the brother Carl 1846 in Mainz

Carl (born 1828), the second son of Anton and Catharina Zahn, trained as a shoemaker in Mainz on the Rhine.
It can be only this Carl, brother of Anton Zahn. The author has not found another of a suitable age at familysearch.org.

From 1846 to 1848 Carl sits two years in the penitentiary. It was probably the one in the Weintorstraße, between the seminary in the Augustinerstraße and the Rhine. Until October 1888, Weintorstrasse was still called Zuchthaustraße. It is also a popular neighborhood for taverns and prostitution.

Carl Zahn was brought before the Assisengericht in Mainz at the age of 18 (when Anton was five) and sentenced for allegedly seducing and abusing the 4.5-year-old daughter of the Mainz shoemaker Ferdinand Zucchi (e.g. in the address book of the city of Mainz later also: Zucky), certainly his instructor and master, into fornication.

There is a second "Zucchi" in the address book of the city of Mainz 1846. This Ch. Zucchi is a portrait painter. From the year 1872 there is no more Zuc(c)hi or Zucky in the Mainz address book.

He can "forget" this education, tick it off. Maybe he is identical with a station attendant Carl Zahn in Frei-Laubersheim, who is mentioned in 1853 and 1862. But this is only speculation. A Carl Zahn born in Germany in 1828 emigrated to the USA in 1853. That could be, is more likely to be him.

The conviction in Mainz, which certainly does not go undetected by relatives and villagers in Gau-Bickelheim, takes place on October 20, 1846 before the Assisengericht Mainz.

His younger brother Anton Zahn, the alleged Jack the Ripper, will be sentenced 17 years later, on October 20, 1863, also by the Assisengericht in Mainz, to five years for theft.

It is the same day of the year (October 20) and even the same day of the week (Tuesday)!

The term "Assisen" is taken from France. Above it there are still the district court and the higher court in Mainz.

Because the crime of Carl Zahn was committed in Mainz or Rheinhessen, he is sentenced by the court there. Because he did not commit murder, he is not sent, for example, to the Marienschloß prison in Rockenberg near Münzenberg in Upper Hesse (Giessen, Wetterau).

However, the author has not found any specific reference to either Carl or Anton Zahn as to which penitentiary the two brothers had to serve their sentence in.

If there was no overcrowding, then it will probably have been the penitentiary in the old town of Mainz in the Weintorstraße.

In many medical books, psychology books and also in the standard work on hypnosis there is talk about three important phases of a young child: oral, anal and the grasping of the own sexual organs. The development of sexuality takes place at about five years of age. Malicious damage to the child's development by adults (or adolescents) in a five-year-old child can and usually does result in damaged, abnormal sexual behavior later in life.

At that time, children in Gau-Bickelheim and elsewhere went to the village school at age six and were thus placed in public, official care. There was no kindergarten yet. Even in the generation of the author of this book, about 30% of the children in the countryside were not in kindergarten. If Anton Zahn acquired a disturbed relationship to sexuality, then 1846 at the age of five is the "best opportunity" to do so, through relatives, acquaintances or strangers, that is, in private. It was not until the age of six that a child was usually sent to regular religious services. Because of the sensitive subconscious before the age of six, from ancient times until the 19th century, children were not given away until they were six years old. However, neither in the private nor in the public sphere one is immune to the fact that an unwanted damage remains in the child.

In addition to the parents' failure to emigrate to Australia in 1840, the little boy is now almost certainly credited with the imprisonment of his brother Carl. "His birth in 1841 is to blame for many things." He is to blame, although he can do nothing for it. Here, in addition to the brother, aunt and cousins would also come into play again.

A second possibility runs on a completely different direction. The special pattern of Anton Zahn to be able to kill a woman (born in his age, i.e. 1840s) only when he is alone with her would have to mean that at the age of about five years the little boy had a similar experience with a girl in his village.

Would it now be presumptuous of the author to believe that Anton's brother Carl Zahn made him keen on a girl of the same age and something went wrong? Was the girl physically hurt by the five-year-old Anton, possibly with a knife, incited by his brother Carl, who was perhaps cheeky but certainly soured because of the conviction in Mainz?

Did this pattern occur at the age of five just before his brother Carl Zahn was arrested, or did it occur shortly after his release at the age of seven?

Did Carl Zahn have a bad influence on his brother Anton because of the history in Mainz or independently of it? Was it a fundamental abnormality of Carl Zahn or did he turn little Anton against other little girls with bad advice out of anger after his imprisonment?

According to familysearch.org, Wilhelmina Francisca Maria Louise Zucchi, born on March 21, 1842 and baptized three days later in St. Stephan in Mainz, was the only (!) child of the couple Ferdinand A. (Anton?) Zucchi and Catharina née Bauer. It almost seems that the Zucchi's overreacted when their apprentice Carl Zahn made a pass at their daughter. But there is no way to prove that. Was it just a nice long talk with the little girl or was it already a little more?

Ferdinand A. Zucchi and Catharina née Bauer were married on Jan. 10, 1836 at St. Ignaz in Mainz. He was baptized on 11 March 1808 in St. Stephan. His father was Carl Anton Wilhelm Zucchi and his grandfather was Anton Maria Zucchi.

After all, the only child W.F.M.L. Zucchi (with the four abbreviated first names she is called in the court record) married and had children in spite of the more or less strong trauma she experienced through Carl Zahn from Gau-Bickelheim in Mainz.

On Feb. 19, 1870, she married Franz Seraphim Koeth, who had been baptized in St. Ignaz on July 29, 1839, in St. Ignaz Church in Mainz. The groom's parents were Johann Andreas

Koeth and Anna Maria née Krick, who had married on 1 January 1834 (New Year's Day) in St. Ignaz Church in Mainz.

Seraphim means "the burning ones" and was probably more commonly used as a given name in the 19th century. St. Francis of Assisi, according to tradition, received the stigmata through a seraph. The orders of the Franciscans and the (poor) Poor Clares are called seraphic orders.

By 1874, four girls were born to the couple, all baptized at St. Ignaz in Mainz:

- Catharina Christina Koeth (born Jan. 2, 1871).
- Catharina Christina Koeth (born Feb. 18, 1872)
- Anna Maria Augustina Koeth (born Aug. 28, 1873)
- Anna Maria Remigius Koeth (born Oct. 1, 1874)
A fanatically religious person could unfairly claim that there is a connection between the demolition of the church in Gau-Bickelheim in 1842 and the year of birth of Mrs. Zucchi in Mainz.

Aunt emigrates to the USA with her son

In the middle of the 19th century, the residences of the inhabitants of the USA were counted every 10 years (Census). So it was a census.
Therefore we learn that a Catherine Helena Becker née Zahn (aunt of Anton Zahn) had her residence in the small settlement of Wheatland in 1850 and in 1860.
Wheatland is part of Kenosha County. This county is the most southeastern "county" in the U.S. state of Wisconsin (capital Madison, largest city Milwaukee). Thus, the county is located on one of the Great Lakes and closest to the city of Chicago, which is part of the U.S. state of Illinois.

Catherine Helena Becker died Dec. 17, 1869, in Wheatland at age 80 and was buried three days later in New Munster, just south (also Kenosha County).

With her husband Franz Becker, who probably died before the birth of their last child Jacob in July 1823, in late 1822 (according to a private link on familysearch.org), she had seven children, two of whom died immediately or a few years after birth. Franz Becker, whom she had married in Gau-Bickelheim in 1811, was the son of Heinrich Becker and Catharina née Eder. The remaining five children were three girls and two boys. Two of the girls Anna Maria and Catharina married (as mentioned) in Gau-Bickelheim in 1840 and had children from 1841.

Son Johann Becker (born August 18, 1813) died in 1881 in Todd County in the U.S. state of Minnesota. When he emigrated is not entirely clear. Most likely together with his mother. Johann married an Anna Christina née Leuker in 1848 or shortly before. She died on Dec. 15, 1868 in the USA. Anton Zahn's cousin has a total of seven children with his wife between Dec. 28, 1848 and Sept. 3, 1868. The oldest child John Francis Becker dies at age 46 in 1895, and the youngest child dies on Oct. 7, 1942.

On Google Maps, one can see the following about Wheatland. The settlement and the neighboring town of New Munster to the south (within quick walking distance) are both on the Fox River and 30 kilometers west of the city of Kenosha. The cemetery in New Munster, where Catharina Helena Becker née Zahn was buried, is clearly visible in Google Maps and is located next to the church.

Both places can be reached from Kenosha on the Lake on road No. 50. The road runs south past Wheatland, but goes directly through New Munster. The cemetery is also located on it. In New Munster the road is called Geneva Road.

Another 20 kilometers west on road No. 50 (it is not an Interstate road, but only one category lower) you come to the small Lake Geneva.

Between Kenosha and New Munster, Road No. 50 is intersected by Interstate 41 (Highway 94) and by Interstate 45. Bristol is located on Interstate 45. Five miles north of Bristol is Paris. Both towns are also in the U.S. state of Wisconsin.

So what should be considered coincidence and what should be considered intentional?

The first ever woman doctor in the Western industrialized world, Elizabeth Blackwell, was born near Bristol, England. She finally found a place at Geneva College after 12 attempts. In Paris, where she had also tried to open a practice or do research, they did not recognize her doctoral degree.

Part of the German Federal Road No. 50 runs from Simmern in the Hunsrück to Rheinböllen. The last part goes from Bingen via Gensingen and finally ends at a crossroad leading from Wöllstein to Gau-Bickelheim, directly at the highway A61. Was the B50 already called that back then? A B41 runs along the Nahe River past Bad Kreuznach and ends just before Bingen on the Rhine.

Interstate 41: Anton Zahn was born in 1841.
Interstate 45: 1845 or 1846 there are problems with Carl Zahn

Maybe a little too much is interpreted into it.
But if there is something to it, then the aunt of Anton Zahn settled with full intention in admiration of Elizabeth Blackwell exactly in this area, at least if one assumes that first only the state Wisconsin was an option. Can this prove the admiration of great female figures by Catharina Becker née Zahn (1789 - 1869)?

Confirmation by Bishop Ketteler 1853

It can be assumed that Anton Zahn was confirmed by Bishop Ketteler of Mainz in Gau-Bickelheim in 1853, i.e. at the age of 12.

That the Westphalian Wilhelm Emmanuel Freiherr von Ketteler, related to the bishop of Münster, Count von Galen, who was courageous during the Hitler era, was in Gau-Bickelheim in 1853 for the consecration of the newly built church is vouched for. (see literature to it or under www.regionalgeschichte.net).

The Catholic parish church of Gau-Bickelheim stands on the Palmberg, at the southern exit of the village and beyond the federal road 420. It was built between 1845 and 1853 according to the plans of the district architect Ludwig Rhumbler and is dedicated to St. Martin.
On June 29, 1853, the new church was consecrated by the great social bishop of Mainz, Ketteler.
On this occasion Ketteler will also have performed the sacrament of confirmation.
The parish priest of Gau-Bickelheim at that time was Jakob Brisbois (1848 - 1855).

At www.regionalgeschichte.net it is said:

Ketteler, who chose the way of the church late, was a friendly person accompanied by outbursts of anger. On March 15, 1850, he was elected Bishop of Mainz. As early as 1851, the Congregation of the Sisters of Divine Providence was founded in Finthen, serving as teachers and nurses. Orphanages were established. The Brothers of Mary, called in 1852, devoted themselves to teaching at the Willigis Gymnasium in Mainz.

Now, for Anton Zahn, perhaps comes a clue that made his anger rise a notch higher: The Women of the Good Shepherd opened a home for at-risk girls in 1853. Ketteler might have included that in his sermon in Gau-Bickelheim.

Only on July 25, 1869, one year after Anton Zahn's release from the Mainz penitentiary, there is a similar case. Perhaps Anton Zahn learned this from the newspaper.

In 1869, Bishop Ketteler gave an address on the Liebfrauenheide near Offenbach am Main, in front of 10 thousand workers. This address is often referred to as the "Magna Charta of the Christian Workers' Movement". Ketteler called for an increase in the working wage, shorter working hours, the guarantee of Sunday rest and the prohibition of child labor in factories. Young girls and pregnant women should enjoy protection and also not work.

Karl Marx and other communists contemptuously dismiss the social work of the churches and assume that the idea was stolen from the communists.

Death of the father in 1855

The next drastic experience was the death of his father in November 1855 at the age of 55. Anton Zahn was 14 years old at the time. Anton Zahn senior was buried by the Catholic priest Franz Blum (1855 - 1873) in Gau-Bickelheim.

This is where the numbers game might have started in Anton Zahn's head: The number "five".

Later, he will serve five years in the penitentiary, from 1863 to 1868. The number "five" also plays a major role in the Whitechapel murders of 1888.

The poverty of the family of the deceased Anton Zahn senior may now have increased. After all, his son Johann (born 1833) emigrated to the USA in 1855.

The fact that Anton must have taken a job as a servant in or around Gau-Bickelheim before 1863 confirms the increasing impoverishment of the family. There is no money left to finance an apprenticeship, as had been the case with his brother Carl (apprenticeship with a shoemaker in Mainz). At that time and for a long time later, the apprentices still had to pay for their apprenticeship themselves. Today they even get money. The middle way would be only purely arithmetically considered in between.

One year earlier, on August 10, 1854, the eldest brother Jacob Zahn (born 1826) married Maria Fides née Beck.

Anton Zahn – in prison

Penitentiary for theft 1863-1868

In the Grand Ducal Government Gazette from the Grand Duchy of Hesse-Darmstadt, which rather resembles a book of medium size, are published in 1864 (among many statistics and announcements of the government) the convicts of the year 1863 from the courts in Darmstadt, Mainz and Giessen.

It says there under the section "Assisengericht zu Mainz": "Anton Zahn, servant of Gau-Bickelheim, for excellent theft, by sentence of 20 Oct. 1863 to a penitentiary sentence of five years."

In the government gazette of 1847, Anton's brother Carl was listed. There, under the section "Assisengericht zu Mainz" it states:
"Carl Zahn, shoemaker apprentice from Gau-Böckelheim, for seduction to fornication by sentence of 20 Oct. 1846 to a penal servitude of two years."

The sentence for theft varied from one year to 18 years. It is not that women would be favored over men here, or vice versa. The sentences themselves seem to vary widely for the same offense.
Other offenses besides theft include fornication, seduction of minors, vagrancy, murder, manslaughter, forgery, and infanticide.

It was the case at the time that manslaughter sometimes carried a lesser penalty than theft. Even in the case of murder, the announced death penalty was not necessarily carried out, and the murderer or murderess was even released from prison after many years. It was probably quite a liberal time.

If a mother killed her child, however, she had to expect at least 10 years in prison.

So Anton Zahn had stolen (not necessarily in Gau-Bickelheim), was a servant, and at the age of 22 was locked away for five years most likely in the penitentiary in the Weintorstraße in Mainz.

It should be noted, however, that an Elisabetha Görlipp, servant girl from Jacobsweiler (in the Rhine Palatinate), then Kingdom of Bavaria, was sentenced for "excellent" theft by judgment of October 21, 1863, only to a sentence in the corrective house of one year and six months "with sharpening" by the Assisengericht in Mainz.

The question is, of course, what in detail has been committed. Only it is somewhat strange that only one day later a woman for the same legal offense of the "excellent theft" does not even get the penitentiary, but only the correction house, and in addition still with a substantially shorter term of imprisonment.

Shouldn't the rage of Anton Zahn against certain women increase immeasurably here?

Prison near Maria Dolorosa & brothel district

The Mainzer Zuchthaus (prison) in the Weintorstraße (until Oct. 1888 Zuchthausstraße) is located between the large Maria Dolorosa chapel in the north and the Mainz brothel district in the Kappelhofgasse in the south.

Surely this should have a tremendous significance!

On the one hand Anton Zahn could have been exposed to the abuse of prostitutes, on the other hand Maria Dolorosa is depicted on paintings with seven swords pierced or with a visible heart.

For a man with oblique sexual fantasies, a tension is created here that the swords of Maria Dolorosa (Mater Maria Dolorosa = the sorrowful Mother of God Mary) is willing to stab into the prostitutes at the best opportunity.

It is possible that the head of the seminary, Markus Adam Nickel, often preached a sermon against prostitution in the Maria Dolorosa chapel opposite the penitentiary. The similarity of the name with the London murder victim Mary Ann Nichols cannot be denied.

A plaque by Burkhart Zamels (* around 1690; + 1757 in Mainz) with a picture and a saying still hangs on the former penitentiary.

The picture shows wild boars, lions and deer pulling a vehicle that brings women to the penitentiary.

The inscription states:

"One does not hurry so fast with your judgment cases, the imperfection has still many companions. Consider beforehand, can you do something better, the censure of this work, otherwise they will laugh at you."

The Maria Dolorosa Chapel between Weintorstrasse and Mauritzenplatz was formerly a Capuchin church. The Capuchins also lived according to the teachings of St. Francis of Assisi.

The seven sorrows of the Mother of Jesus are:

1. Mary is prophesied the fate of her son
2. flight to Egypt from the child murderer Herod
3. Mary loses her 12 years old son in the temple
4. Jesus meets his mother at the way of the cross
5. crucifixion and death of Christ
6. taking down of the cross and handing over of the body to Mary
7. entombment of Christ

In contrast to the Maria Dolorosa, there is the Maria Letitia. The seven joys are:

1. the Annunciation
2. the Visitation
3. the birth of Jesus
4. the adoration of the wise men
5. the finding of the 12 years old Jesus in the temple
6. the resurrection of Jesus
7. the bodily assumption into heaven.

Among other things, the day in the church year when a memorial to the Sorrows (Dolorosa) of Mary is held is amazing. It is the 15th of September.

This day is about exactly halfway between August 31, 1888 (1st Jack the Ripper murder) or September 1, 1894 (Anton Zahn's murder in the USA) and September 30, 1888 (3rd & 4th Jack the Ripper murders).

Acquaintances in prison

The big questions now are:

- Who among his fellow inmates could have persuaded Anton Zahn to become a sailor on the high seas?
- Who could have made strangulation and throat slitting palatable to him in prison?
- Through which stories of inmates could the hatred have been sown especially for English women?

The exact same terms 1863 to 1868 as Anton Zahn have:
- August Strauß, servant at Udenheim, sentenced on April 20, 1863, to five years in prison for grievous bodily harm resulting in death. (On April 11, the newspaper "Rheinhessischer Beobachter" had still reported that the defendant was on the run).
- August Kirchner, roper apprentice at Mainz, sentenced to five years in prison for robbery on July 21, 1863.

There are at least 40 prisoners for whom the periods of imprisonment at least barely overlap. It would be rather tedious to go through each individual.

The journeyman locksmith Philipp Emrich from Worms had stabbed a maid to death and stood trial with August Strauß. Also on trial were a maid from Mainz who had killed her child and a basket maker from Mainz who had accidentally killed the son of the spice merchant Wagner by throwing a stone during a quarrel.

Even women are not immune to murder and manslaughter:
- Elisabeth Butterfaß from Pfeddersheim near Worms, sentenced to 14 years in prison for manslaughter by the Assisengericht in Mainz on Oct. 25, 1855.

However, one of Anton Zahn's fellow inmates stands out in particular:
- Wilhelm Eisenhardt, ship's servant (probably in Mainz), came from Grombach (Baden), sentenced on 16 Oct. 1861 by the Assisengericht in Mainz to five years in prison for seduction and abuse for fornication.

"Grombach" does not sound like anything special at first. First of all, it is a village in the Heilbronn district and has belonged to the town of Bad Rappenau since 1973.
While Heilbronn belonged to Württemberg in the 19th century, Bad Rappenau and Grombach were Baden.
In the corner there is also a former exclave of Hesse-Darmstadt, the city of Bad Wimpfen (1803 - 1945). That is why Bad Wimpfen still belongs to the diocese of Mainz, because the dioceses in Germany are still oriented to the national borders of 1816. Thus, there is already a reference to the city of Mainz.
But the inconspicuous Grombach has other treasures to offer.
Friedrich Anton von Venningen (Oct. 13, 1765 - May 7, 1832), who owned Grombach and the castle there, was chief bailiff in (Bad) Kreuznach on the Nahe, royal Bavarian chamberlain and privy councilor, lord of Grombach and director of the theater in Mannheim.
His son Karl Theodor von Venningen-Ullner (1806 - 1874) married in November 1833 in Munich the English "Lebefrau" (as in bon vivant) Jane Digby. With her he was for a short time in Grombach, when he started the renovation of the castle.

Anton Zahn – from 1869

At his aunt's funeral in USA 1869?

Between his release from the penitentiary in Mainz in 1868 at the age of 27 and the murders in London in 1888 at the age of 47, it is now impossible to see what Anton Zahn did with his life. Perhaps he first traveled a lot to relieve the frustration of prison. Possibly his brothers gave him money so that he could do this.

Possibly Anton Zahn attends the funeral of his aunt Catharina Becker née Zahn on Dec. 20, 1869 in Wisconsin, USA. His father's sister had died on Dec. 17.
He may have even attended the funeral of his aunt's daughter-in-law a year earlier. Anna Christina Becker née Leuker died on Dec. 15, 1868 in the USA.

Death of mother in 1876 in Gau-Bickelheim

In October 1876 Catharina Zahn née Zahn dies as widow of Anton Zahn (senior).
All of her sons and daughter Magdalena are probably still alive and may have all traveled to the funeral in Gau-Bickelheim, including relatives in the USA and in Hofheim near Bensheim.

Anton Zahn – 1888 in London?

Jack the Rippers victims in London

The following five women are counted as victims of "Jack the Ripper" in London:

1. Mary Ann Nichols (Aug. 26, 1845 - Aug. 31, 1888)
2. Annie Chapman (ca. 1841 - September 8, 1888)
3. Elizabeth Stride (Nov. 27, 1843 - Sept. 30, 1888)
4. Catherine Eddowes (April 14, 1842 - Sept. 30, 1888)
5. Mary Jane Kelly (ca. 1863 - Nov. 9, 1888)

London surgeon Thomas Bond, after being commissioned by Robert Anderson, head of Scotland Yard's crime-solving division, to draw up a profile of the perpetrator, stated that the murderer "must have had no knowledge of either a surgeon or a butcher, he must have been a loner, with intermittent outbursts of destructive and sexual mania."
Further, according to Bond, it must be assumed that the "destructive drive" developed from a "vindictive or brooding state of mind." Alternatively, a "religious mania" is also conceivable as a trigger.

Only two murders occurred in the Whitechapel neighborhood. All five victims lived in the Spitalfields neighborhood to the northwest, and three of the five murders were committed there.

Known to many only as "Whitechapel." Possibly because that is where the first murder occurred.
There are three murders (Chapman, Kelly and Eddowes) between "Catherine's Dock" (harbor) and the Spitalfields market hall, newly built in 1887 in the London district of the same name.

The infamous "Jack the Ripper" murders in the autumn of 1888 in the Whitechapel district of London (east of the city center, north of the Thames) claimed five female victims, all prostitutes who carried out this activity full-time or part-time, according to police investigators at the time.

The British ex-detective Trevor Marriott assumes that the murderer could be a German sailor, who was always up to mischief on weekends from the London dock "Catherine's Dock" south of Whitechapel.

According to Marriott, documents from London's port authorities indicate that a sailor on the German merchant ship "Reiher" (engl. Heron) could be the perpetrator in three of the five murders between August 31 and November 9, 1888, in which the women's throats were slit with a six-inch knife. The women were strangled before and after that the internal organs were mutilated.

On Aug. 31, Sept. 8 and Nov. 9, this very steamer "Reiher" of the North German Lloyd (NDL) based in Bremen was in London's port "Catherine's Dock." However, not at the double murder on September 30, 1888. The reason, according to the researchers, was that the ship "Reiher" had a collision with another ship on the Thames in the meantime and had to be repaired. On September 30, however, the ship "Sperber" of the NDL was lying in the harbor basin "Catherine's Dock" as a substitute.

Among the many people suspected of being "Jack the Ripper" at the time was a German named Carl Feigenbaum, who had been arrested for a murder in New York on Sept. 1, 1894.

Anton Zahn, sentenced to death in the U.S. under his alias Carl Feigenbaum, is among 13 people suspected of being "Jack the Ripper" either by the London police or by lawyers and authorities in England or the U.S. at the time.

Anton Zahn is the only German among the suspects. And he is the only one who did not have a permanent residence in 1888, when the Jack the Ripper murders were committed in Whitechapel and Spitalfields, because he was a sailor. The rest are citizens of the British Empire or the United States of America. Some are London-based migrants from Eastern Europe, including those of the Jewish faith.

First murder

What struck the author (of this book) about the last murder of Anton Zahn alias Carl Ferdinand Feigenbaum:
Why does he take the risk of being caught by the 16-year-old son of the murdered Juliane Hoffman in New York in 1894? He disregards all caution.
In all the previous murders, Anton Zahn admits to further murders in the USA after all, and according to his testimony he was in London in 1888, he certainly avoided the risk that a third party might reveal his identity to the police.
Zahn is extremely obsessed with killing a woman around August 31 of all days.
In the first murder on August 31, 1888, the murderer tries to make everything perfect after all.

Every year, each day on the calendar moves forward one day of the week. In the case of a leap year, it skips a weekday.
Because between August 1888 and August 1894 exactly one leap year, i.e. 1890, lies in between, the 31st of August, which fell in 1888 on a Friday, falls in 1894 again on a Friday.

That's exactly six years apart (the week has seven days), and the author wouldn't be surprised if the number six in this context has to do with "sex," the abbreviation for sexuality.

Markus Adam Nickel & Mary Ann Nichols

Anton Zahn's home village of Gau-Bickelheim, like Bingen, Gau-Algesheim and Heidesheim, as well as the Rheingau, belonged to the Electorate of Mainz until around 1800. In contrast, Ingelheim, Bad Kreuznach, Simmern, Oppenheim, Horrweiler, etc. belonged to the Electoral Palatinate.

Now it is written e.g. in the books of the GDR scientist Heinrich Scheel about the Mainz Republic that Gau-Bickelheim had belonged to the Mainz seminary in particular and was probably still looked after by it at times in the 19th century.

As a second point one can probably assume that the seminary in the time when Anton Zahn was in the penitentiary in Mainz from 1863 to 1868, held masses in the chapel Maria Dolorosa next to it, during which groups of prison inmates were probably led there one after the other from the opposite side of the Zuchthausgasse (from Oct. 1888 Weintorstraße) with guards.

The seminary has been located in Augustinergasse since the 19th century, only a few steps away from the Zuchthaus (prison).

Markus Adam Nickel (* June 9, 1800 in Mainz; + Oct. 31, 1869 in Mainz) was provost ("regent") of the Mainz seminary from 1835 to 1851, according to Wikipedia.

The seminary is located at Augustinerstrasse 34; next to it nestles the seminary church, architecturally built similarly to

155

the Ignazkirche, with the interior in shades of pink instead of light green.

According to the editor Friedhelm Jürgensmeier of the book "Das Bistum Mainz" (The Diocese of Mainz), Markus Adam Nickel was for many years a teacher at the episcopal high school in Mainz and then professor of moral theology and precisely Regens (Regent) of the seminary.
M.A. Nickel was above all a link, i.e. a bridge between the first and the second Mainz school of theologians. He is convincing as a theological author in the effort, so it says further, "in continuation of the practical work of his models" Liebermann and Bishop Colmar to show ways of piety oriented to the Bible.
M.A. Nickel is not to be confused with Joseph Nickel (1802 - 1855). Joseph Nickel was a cathedral priest. He was asked by Wilhelm Emmanuel Ketteler, at that time not yet bishop in Mainz, probably about 1848, to hold the social question in energetic style at the Advent sermons in the Mainz Cathedral. At least that is how it is reported in Jürgensmeier's book.

Markus Adam Nickel, ordained a priest in 1823 according to Wikipedia, was appointed professor of theology and spiritual director at the Mainz seminary in 1830. In 1833, according to Wikipedia, he is said to have become cathedral pastor (Is this confused with Joseph Nickel; or were the persons successively cathedral pastors?).
In 1835, the Bishop of Mainz, P.L. Kaiser, appointed M.A. Nickel as regent of the seminary and as spiritual councilor. After resigning the presidency of the seminary, M.A. Nickel was elected cathedral chaplain in 1851. As such, he taught homiletics and liturgy at the seminary almost until the end of his life in 1869.

Thus, while M.A. Nickel was the "Regent" (or "Regens") of the seminary only from 1835 to 1851, beyond that he was closely associated with the seminary from 1830 until his death in late 1869.

The similarity of first name and last name between this Mark Adam Nickel and the first official Jack the Ripper victim Mary Ann Nichols is striking!

Anton Zahn met this important man either in Gau-Bickelheim or as a prisoner in Mainz and heard him preach. This is to be assumed.

M.A. Nickel also publishes several books. Thus there are the following writings of him:

- "The holy times and feasts according to their history and celebration in the church," 1836, new edition 1863, 6 vols.
- "The New Testament. Purpose, plan and dissection of all the individual books", 1846, 4 vols.
- "The Gospel Pericopes, exegetically-homiletically edited," 1847-1854, 18 volumes (Gospel in the sense of "Gospels in the New Testament")
- "Beredsamkeit der Kirchenväter nach Jos. Weissenbach," 1844, 4 volumes, edited together with Joseph Kehrein (* Oct. 20, 1808 Heidesheim am Rhein; + March 25, 1876 in Montabaur)
- "Summa der mystischen Theologie oder des gottseligen Thomas von Kempis vier Bücher von der Nachfolge Christi, systematisch geordnet nach den drei Wegen Reinigung, Erleuchtung und Vereinigung", 1851.

Joseph Kehrein is also found in Wikipedia: He was a German teacher, philologist, historian, and director of the Montabaur Teacher's Seminary. 1823 Attended the Bischöfl. Gymnasium in Mainz, 1831 to 1834 studied classical philology in Giessen. He also studied philosophy, art history, mathematics, English and French. In 1845 he was appointed by Schulrat Dr. Gottfried Seebode to the Gymnasium in Hadamar (near Limburg an der Lahn) and worked there for ten years as deputy director. In 1855 he was appointed director of the teacher training college in Montabaur.

Concerning our Jack the Ripper candidate Anton Zahn (alias Carl Ferdinand Feigenbaum) the following speculations would be possible, which I made in 2015, years before I discovered the codes in London:

- The name Markus Adam Nickel could possibly have meaning for Anton Zahn.
- The first Jack the Ripper murder victim Mary Ann Nichols [pronounced "Nikels"] might have had the misfortune to have a rather similar name to Markus Adam Nickel.
- Version 1: Anton Zahn is on the side of Markus Adam Nickel. He sees how the prostitutes in London live extremely contrary to the teachings of M.A. Nickel.
- Version 2: Anton Zahn is not on the side of Markus Adam Nickel. He takes revenge on him posthumously by vicariously killing Mary Ann Nichols.
- Version 3: Quite improbable would be if Anton Zahn had suffocated M.A. Nickel in Mainz with a pillow on Oct. 31, 1869, for example, and had similarly killed his aunt in Wisconsin (USA) on Dec. 17, 1869.

The 1869 murders would have to be ruled out immediately if the priest and the aunt died in the presence of third parties, and Anton Zahn was definitely not present.
Just in 1869, the women's movement in the U.S. had advanced quite a bit. And Anton Zahn was released from the penitentiary in Mainz at the end of 1868.

If 1888 was Anton Zahn's first murder, then the Rhenishman falls into the small minority of serial killers who do not start murdering until they are over 45 years old. In 1869 he was 28 years old.

Unfortunately, today we can no longer reconstruct what Markus Adam Nickel recited in the masses. But at least it is possible to have a look into his books.

In "Summa der mystischen Theologie oder des gottseligen Thomas von Kempis vier Bücher von der Nachfolge Christi, systematisch geordnet nach den drei Wegen Reinigung, Erleuchtung und Vereinigung" (Summa of Mystical Theology or of the Blessed Thomas von Kempis Four Books of the Discipleship of Christ, Systematically Arranged According to the Three Paths of Purification, Enlightenment, and Union) from 1851, the following sentences can be found on the keywords "woman(s)," "woman," "knife," and "instincts."

Terms "women" and "woman":

P.279f.

< 112. Step: With which people one should avoid confidences, with which one should cultivate them?

I. One must avoid intimacy with young people, strangers and the rich; II. with the female sex; III. on the other hand, one must desire and cultivate it with God and the blessed spirits.

I. Be seldom with young people and strangers; do not flatter the rich, and do not appear gladly before the great; be with the humble and the simple, with the pious and the well-behaved; and what belongs to edification, negotiate with them.

B.1.ch.8.§.1.

II. Be not confidential against any woman; but commend all godly women to God in general. B.1.ch.8.§.1.7

III. To be confidential with God alone and with His angels; but for the sake of mankind depart from love one must have for all; but confidentiality is not pious.
B.1.ch.8.§.1.2. >

S.792
< ... So you are the teacher of the apostles and among three women you have been distinguished as the most famous, as the first. ... >

Term "instincts":

P.316f.
< 136. Step: The desires of the heart must be examined and tempered.

I. Notice well where these desires aim - whether at God, whether at yourself? II. We must therefore use prudence III. sometimes even force.

I. ... Often desires inflame you and drive you violently; but consider whether you are moved more for My glory > (God, Jesus or the like) < or your benefit. ...
B.3.ch.11.§.1.

II.
... For not every impulse that seems good should be followed at once; but also not every contrary impulse should be fled at once.
B.3.ch.11.§.2.

At times force must be used, and the sensual urge of desire must be met in a manly way; nor must one pay attention to what the flesh wants and what it does not want; but rather strive to make it subject to the spirit even against its will; and so long must it be chastised and forced to be under bondage, until it is ready for everything and learns to be content with little, and to enjoy simple things; nor even grumble against anything inconvenient.
B. 3.ch. 11. §.3. >

Term "woman": (an example)

S.756f.
< Third prayer
To the blessed Virgin Mary, for obtaining a special consolation.
Merciful Mother of God Mary, graciously receive your servant and servant to yourself, ...Most loving Virgin, ... Behold, my wife and mistress, upon my many sufferings and open to me the womb of your grace and mercy. ... >

Term "knife":

Page xxiii:
< But he who wants to anatomize the feeling of the heart and the language of feeling with the cold knife of understanding, and otherwise wants nothing but to anatomize, has as little the right mood to read the book as your friend would have the right mood to suffer with you at the death of your child, if he wanted to anatomize the corpse and seek out the cause of the disease in the constituent parts of the body before your eye.

As a teacher of the art of dissection, he does well when he wants to dissect; but when he wants to dissect where he should sympathize, he is in the wrong place with all his art of dissection. Thus the cold, correctly dissecting mind is a beautiful gift for this earth; but when the mind wants to cut and divide with its knife, where the heart should feel and be brought by feeling to the recognition of the true and great, then the mind with all its art of dissection is in the wrong place. >

It may be that Anton Zahn has reinterpreted some things. After all, he has been able to be patient (to say it with bitter irony) for 20 years after 1868 or 1869, before he starts to strike in 1888. But the explanations of Markus Adam Nickel are already somewhat misleading and unclear. The many repetitions seem like prayer wheels, which could bring some listeners into a kind of frenzy.

Two heirs of the 1888 house in Pfaffen-Schwabenheim

Helena Diegel née Wetzel   *Anna Elis. Kolb née Diegel*
(1882-1941)   *(1904-1956)*

I thank Gertrud Sonntag née Diegel (1907-1989), the sister of my grandmother, for the left photo; Right picture is private property

Disappeared documents

Crew lists of 1888 in Bremen

The British ex-investigator Trevor Marriott reports in his 2005 book and in his film that he also searched for "Carl Feigenbaum" (or for another meaningful name) in the Seemannsarchiv in Bremen.

He went through year by year. When he then wanted to look at the year 1888, he had to find out that it was no longer available in the Bremen archive.

Because Marriott wanted to know who was registered as crew, as sailors, on the ship "Reiher" and the ship "Sperber" on the voyages from Bremen to London in the fall of 1888.
Marriott suspects Attorney Lawton in New York may have borrowed the 1888 and not returned it.
It may have been other people who did not want a German to have the dubious honor of being Jack the Ripper.
The question is whether the archive in Bremen itself can trace when this year went missing and who might have rummaged through the records.

Court minutes Okt. 1863 in Mainz

The author of this book was at first astonished that the city archives in Mainz still possessed the loose sheets in two cartons, whereupon a scribe briefly summarized the results of the criminal trials in the three Mainz courts, Assisengericht, Bezirksgericht and Obergericht.
Now the author had first "taken care" of Anton's brother Carl.

On sheet no. 6 R 5015 I.a. dated October 6, 1846 with the pre-printed heading "Der General-Staatsprocurator am Großherzoglich Hessischen Obergerichte der Provinz Rheinhessen" (The General State Procurator at the Grand Ducal Hessian High Court of the Province of Rhine Hesse), two cases are entered, announced on September 21 and October 5.

1) Friedrich Geimer, journeyman cooper, committed "excellent" theft to the "detriment" of D. Futzi at Mainz.

2) Carl Zahn from "Gauböckelheim", apprentice shoemaker at Mainz, is charged with the crime of seduction to fornication and abuse of the person of 4 1/2 years old W.F.M.L. Zuchi, daughter of F. Zuchi at Mainz.

In contrast to the court records of 1863, those of 1846 are extremely legible, provided the reader is proficient in the "Sütterlin" script.
The names of the defendants are even written in the script of "Latin", i.e. like today's handwriting and thus completely legible without any problems.
In the books "Großherzoglich Hessisches Regierungsblatt" of 1847 and of the year 1864 (thus in each case one year after the trial) the sentence and thus the announcement of the sentence with Carl Zahn and with his brother Anton Zahn is set in each case on 20 October.
The disadvantage in the books in contrast to the loose sheets, however, is that the aggrieved parties are not entered.

Therefore the author (of this book) wanted to have a look at the minutes of October 1863 in the loose-leaf collection.
To his horror, he had to discover that the years around 1863 were, first, very difficult to read. While it was a very nice, even script, it was extremely difficult to decipher even with

a good knowledge of "Sütterli" because one letter resembled another.

The only elements that were easily recognizable were the usual preprint in the heading, the date of execution, and a reference at the end to a law of 1852.

Oddly enough, the months were sorted opposite to the years. So if you went from 1862 to 1863, you jumped from January 1862 to December 1863.

It was almost like the Arabic script, where a person not familiar with writing can only read the numbers. But the months in the upper right margin could still be distinguished. For this and in search of the name "Zahn", the author went through the year 1863 five times.

Unfortunately, it had to be determined that the complete October 1863 (at least when the author was in the archives) could not be found!

September was to be read, and then only November again. Also all other months except October were to be found.

Now, probably, as with the 1888 ship lists in Bremen in Mainz, an unknown person took the liberty to let the documents disappear during the court proceedings. Possibly because Anton Zahn is suspected of being Jack the Ripper. The only question is when and who.

Because of the very difficult reading, one cannot sit down tedious minutes to find the entry of Anton Zahn. Is that why the complete October 1863 is missing?

Unlike the District Court and the High Court in Mainz, the Assisengericht only met in the months of January (1st quarter), April (2nd quarter), July (3rd quarter) and October (4th quarter).

It is now no longer traceable to whom Anton Zahn broke in to steal from this victim.

Furthermore, because of this very document (which is no longer or currently untraceable), it can no longer be clarified in which locality Anton Zahn was a servant or where he committed the theft.

Conjectures about Anton Zahn's theft

Because the police protocols on the arrest of Anton Zahn probably also no longer exist, only the newspaper "Rheinhessischer Beobachter" from Ober-Ingelheim, which was published twice a week at that time, remains to at least give conjectures on the theft.

First, the term "excellent" theft should be explained. In Pierer's Universal-Lexicon from the year 1857 the following is written about it:

< Theft with distinction (Furtum qualificatum, Rechtswiss.), in contrast to simple theft (Furtum simplex), is that theft in which the law, because of special additional circumstances that make the thief appear to be an exceptionally deliberate and dangerous criminal, or because of the nature of the stolen object characterize him as a particularly contemptible person, threatens a penalty that exceeds the usual penalties for theft.

According to common criminal law, these include

a) theft with burglary (effractio), when the thief deliberately enters a building by forcibly opening it, be it an ordinary or unusual entrance, in order to obtain the object;

b) theft with entry, when the thief deliberately enters an inhabited or uninhabited building from the outside by climbing, whether up or down, e.g. into a cellar;

c) armed theft, if the thief has intentionally provided himself with tools with which he could inflict bodily injury in the event of resistance, before committing the crime in order to carry out the theft without hindrance;

d) theft from a church (sacrilege), which includes the theft from a consecrated place of a thing intended for religious worship; finally, in general

e) every third theft, no matter if it was a simple or a qualified one.

The punishment of the excellent thefts is, according to the punishable neck court order, generally death, for which, however, by the newer practice arbitrary imprisonment is used. ... >
In the bi-weekly newspaper "Rheinhessischer Beobachter" from Ober-Ingelheim, which brings news from all over Rheinhessen and the world, as well as announcements and advertisements, there are generally no reports of thefts. Usually, apart from more pleasant events, there are only murders or accidents resulting in death.

Even Anton Zahn is mentioned in this newspaper, in the issue of Wednesday, Oct. 7, 1863. There it says in very small print:
< At the assizes of the 4th quarter per 1863 beginning on Oct. 11, the following criminal cases will come to trial: ... 7) Tuesday > 20 Oct. < Indictment against Anton Zahn, farmhand from Gau-Bickelheim, for excellent theft; ... >
The only way to get a clue to a theft are the announcements of auctions or the advertisements. At least one can assume that the theft of Anton Zahn was committed in Rheinhessen, because otherwise the court in Darmstadt would probably be responsible for the province Starkenburg, for example.

The second question, however, is: How long did it take after the crime until the trial at the Assisengericht in Mainz?
The two murder cases in Ober-Ingelheim from 1860 are a clue to this.
The first murder of Mr. Daudistel is in the news shortly after on June 2, 1860. The second murder of Mr. Menck is three days after the crime on Sept. 29, 1860 in the news sheet.

Both murder cases come before the Assisengericht in Mainz in the same session, namely in January (1st quarter) 1861. Thus the first murder by Mr. Stumpf and Mr. Emmert is just over half a year ago and the second murder by Mr. Nichtern just over a quarter of a year ago. Strictly speaking, the first murder is still just in the 2nd quarter of 1860 and the second murder just in the 3rd quarter of 1860.

The question is whether the grand larceny of Anton Zahn could also have occurred at the beginning of the 3rd quarter of 1863, only to be tried as early as the 4th quarter of 1863.

Because interesting is e.g. the edition "Rheinhessischer Beobachter" from 18 July 1863. There it says among other things:

- < Auction at Gau-Bickelheim. Thursday, July 23, 1863, in the morning at 9 o'clock, Dr. Sommer, doctor and landowner in Gau-Bickelheim, leaves in his apartment there because of giving up his oeconomy business:

4 horses, 14 cows, 4 pigs, 1 two-horse chaise, 2 harvest wagons, 2 wheelbarrows, 6 plows, several iron and wooden harrows, 1 roller, 1 windmill, 1 feed mill, carting and farming equipment, as well as all the equipment necessary for the operation of the economy from credit in property auction. Wallertheim, July 14, 1863, Jungk, Grand Ducal Notary. > (Advertisement No. 1423)

- The undersigned brings his stock of hunting rifles and Lefaucheux > (pin-fuse cartridges) < as well as samples of Ordonanzstutzen for on target stands in far greater selection in recommendable memory. J. Zahn in Alzey > (advertisement no. 1443)

In the first case there is an announcement of an auction directly in Gau-Bickelheim, at the doctor Dr. Sommer.

And in the second case it is an advertisement for an Alzey gun store and after all the same family name "Zahn".

Anton Zahn – from 1892 in USA

Resident in Syracuse 1892

Consequently, this was not investigated by Vanderlinden or Marriott: Namely, whether Carl Feigenbaum alias Anton Zahn had a residence in the USA from 1892 on.

Anton and his brother Johann Zahn had stated in 1896 that Anton had given up seafaring at the beginning of 1892 and had traveled a lot in the USA since then.

On the familysearch.org website, the 1892 Census of New York State lists an Anton Zahn, born in Germany in 1841, as residing in Syracuse, a town far north of New York City (south of the Great Lakes).

The designation of the residence is "Syracuse, 12, 06, County Onondaga, U.S. State of New York."

Perhaps we can be sure that this is the Anton Zahn we are looking for if we note that a married Mrs. Zahn from Rheinhessen also lived there. This would make it a similar case to the city of Cincinnati in the US state of Ohio. For there Anton Zahn inherited a legacy in 1894 at the latest. There also lives a married Mrs. Zahn, also from Rheinhessen.

Admittedly, it is a bit daring to be sure here that it is Anton Zahn from Gau-Bickelheim. But "Anton" is not such a common first name as "John" or "Johann". In the case of the brother Johann Zahn (as already written in this book) the month of birth is given in the US census and, moreover, the year of his entry into the USA in 1855 is exactly the year when the father of the two brothers dies.

Well, maybe for the analysis whether Anton Zahn was this ominous Jack the Ripper in London, it is not so important when exactly he entered the USA (finally). But this entry in the Census in Syracuse would confirm the statement of his brother Johann Zahn.

In the source "Hessen HFK deceased in America", in the case of Syracuse, a Margarethe Zahn née Hornung from Alsheim (Rheinhessen) is found. The husband is not listed. She has the destination "America, USA, New York, Syracuse". She dies according to this source in 1899 at the age of 63. Thus, she was born around 1836.

It would have been delightful to discover Anton Zahn in one of the pictures of the Syracuse Fire Department. There are about 15 brigades of about 8 people each with picture and name preserved from those years.

But the stay was probably only 1892 and much too short for that. After all, it is said to have been used on the ships for fire fighting in particular.

Heritage in Cincinnati 1894

According to the source "Hesse HFK who died in America" at the age of 66, an Anne Marie Zahn born Kirch died in 1894 in Cincinnati, Ohio. She came from Bodenheim near Mainz (Rheinhessen). She was born around 1828. Here, too, the husband is not given.

In his will in Sing Sing Prison, shortly before his death, Anton Zahn arranged for his house and apartment in Cincinnati, Ohio to be sold and for the proceeds to go to his sister Magdalena, a widowed straw band in Gau-Bickelheim near Alzey (Rheinhessen).

Because both an Anton Zahn born in 1841 near a Frau Zahn from Rheinhessen in Syracuse is registered in 1892 (year of the final immigration of Anton Zahn to the USA) and another Frau Zahn from Rheinhessen in Cincinnati dies in 1894 (year as Anton Zahn as Carl Feigenbaum is arrested for the murder of Juliane Hoffman in New York), one could assume that both women were visited by Anton Zahn.

Anton Zahn may have inherited from her when Anne Marie Zahn, born Kirch, died. It was precisely this inheritance that he could have bequeathed to his sister Magdalena Strohband in Gau-Bickelheim two years later in the form of money from the sale by the prison or his lawyer.

In familysearch.org we find the woman in a census of the US state Ohio from the year 1870. An Anna M. Zahn, 42 years old, (* around 1828) from Hessen-Darmstadt comes with a 48-year-old Wilhelm) Zahn, who came from "Bavaria", probably from the Rhine Palatinate, which at that time belonged to Bavaria.

The names of the children are a bit strange and could suggest that the family lived in the French metropolis of Paris for a long time or that, apart from the youngest child, they are not their own children, i.e. three out of four children were adopted:

• A. John Paris, 16 years old, male
• Me. O. Paris, 13 years old, male
• Anne C. Paris, 11 years old, female
• Wm (Wilhelm) Zahn, 3 years old, male

Whether Anton Zahn inherited from this family in 1894 is, of course, pure speculation by the author. But maybe there is still one or the other document that confirms or refutes it. The death certificate of Anna Zahn can be found at http: // drc.libraries.uc.edu / with the keyword Cincinnati, Ohio:
Zahn, Anna
Death: 1894-02-07
Address (s): 2 Coppin St.
Age: 66 years, 11 months, 23 days
Born: in Germany
Cause: Cancer of stomach

The death certificate was issued by Dr. J.M. Topmoeller. Then there is the name "Westermann" and the cemetery "St.Marys Cem."
She was born in Bodenheim in 1827.

Anton Zahn bought or inherited a house in Cininnati. After all, there are a few months between February and August 1894 to take over the inheritance. For more detailed informations one would have to go to the archives in Cincinnati.

Anton Zahn – again to 1894/96

Parents - 9 instead of 3 siblings

During court hearings and interrogations by his attorney Lawton between 1894 and 1896, Anton Zahn revealed his true name and origins only very gradually.

Instead of Carl Feigenbaum, his name would be Anton or Carl Zahn (maybe also Zahm). The Briton Trevor Marriott also suspected "Anton Strohband" in his book in 2005, but that would have gone too far.

What is really interesting are the details of the cornered man about his siblings:

Anton Zahn claims to have two sisters, including the widow Magdalena Strohband and a brother Johann Zahn. He doesn't reveal more than he has to.

If you research on the familysearch.org website and, to be on the safe side, in the original church records of the Catholic community of Gau-Bickelheim, you will find that Anton Zahn (baptized May 17, 1841) had two sisters, but:

The older sister Anna Margaretha (baptized August 9, 1830; died November 15, 1832) died as a toddler long before he was born at the age of two.

The younger sister Magdalena (baptized July 31, 1847) married a Heinrich Kaufmann on June 29, 1869. Or it was another Magdalena Zahn from another family.

The Strohband family has existed in Gau-Bickelheim throughout the 19th century. Today it no longer exists.

Anton Zahn cannot deny his brother Johann Zahn either, because Johann had visited him several times in prison, most recently the day before his execution.

In addition, Anton Zahn has five other brothers in his German homeland, which he confidently or defiantly withholds from the US authorities.

Overall, the parents, the father Anton Zahn senior (* April 13, 1800; + November 5, 1855) from Gau-Bickelheim and the mother Katharina born Zahn (* May / June 1801; + October 1876) from Eckelsheim, who married two months before the birth of their first child (!) on June 7, 1826, the following nine children:

• Jacob (baptized 8/9/1826, + after 1840)
• Carl (baptized May 29, 1828, + after 1846)
• Anna Margaretha (*August 9, 1830, +November 15, 1832)
• Johann (* June 29, 1833, + after 1900 in USA)
• Martin (* August 10, 1835, + after 1840)
• Mathias (* July 27, 1838, + after 1840)
• Anton (* May 17, 1841, + April 27, 1896 in USA)
• Joseph (* September 19, 1844)
• Magdalena (* July 31, 1847, + after 1896)

The Anton and Katharina Zahn family from Gau-Bickelheim are planning an officially recorded emigration to Australia in 1840. (see: www.arcinsys.de)

The five sons Jacob, Carl, Johann, Martin and Mathias are still living in this document. Their age is also given when they wish to emigrate, in accordance with the baptism entries in the church register. Only the daughter Anna Margaretha is no longer alive. This also coincides with the entries in the church book.

In contrast to neighboring communities in the vicinity, the desire to emigrate between 1830 and 1860 is extremely high in Gau-Bickelheim. Not all who emigrate are registered in these documents. Conversely, not all who are documented emigrate.

Anton Zahn junior (born and baptized May 17th, 1841) is probably the reason for the failure to emigrate. Both parents die in Gau-Bickelheim.

Anton Zahn senior (1800 - 1855) has a much older sister who emigrated to the USA with her son in the 1840s. Her two daughters, one generation older cousins of Anton Zahn junior (1841 - 1896), stayed back in Germany. These two cousins (bases) married in Gau-Bickelheim in mid-1840.

It looks as if the emigration of Anton Zahn junior's parents and siblings (1841 - 1896) was a foregone conclusion with his aunt and her children.

The relatives remain in Germany. A year before Anton was born, his closest ones should or would have planned to emigrate to Australia.

Now, exactly then, Anton Zahn junior will be born!

Because of the promised inheritance of their grandfather, who was still alive, the cousins married in 1840. Now the uncle Anton Zahn senior remains with his family in Gau-Bickelheim and dangerously diminishes the future fortune. The aunt and the two cousins may indirectly blame the child Anton Zahn junior (born 1841). At least the toddler Anton is the reason why his family doesn't emigrate after all. That's what the aunt will do for the next few years. That at least suggests an enmity between sister Catharina Becker née Zahn (1789 - 1869) and brother Anton Zahn senior (1800 - 1855). But there is another opportunity in 1846, when Anton was five years old, to ruin the little boy's soul.

Anton's older brother Carl Zahn was brought before a court in Mainz at the age of 18 (when Anton was five years old) and sentenced for having seduced and abused a 4.5 years old girl to fornicate.

The cousin Catharina Becker, who married in 1840, was even born and baptized on August 31, 1819. In the church book it says "nata et baptista" on this day (familysearch.org may incorrectly place the birth on August 30th).

On a Saturday, August 31, 1888 and six years later on a Sunday, September 1, 1894, Mary Ann Nichols were murdered in London by Jack the Ripper and Juliana Hoffman in New York by Anton Zahn.

The freedom fighter Mathilde Hitzfeld from Kirchheim-Bolanden was born on September 1st. Perhaps this is also related to the 1894 murder. But only if Anton junior had a special relationship with famous women. But more on that later.

Interview of his brother Johann Zahn

In 1855, when Johann and Anton Zahn's father died, Johann emigrated to the USA. Familysearch.org refers to Johann Zahn, who was born in Germany in June 1833 (after all, the month June is included, especially since John or Johann is a common first name), who lived in 1900 in Borough of Brooklyn, Election District 29, New York City, Ward 22, Kings, New York State, USA, along with his wife Margaret and two sons Frank and Joseph.

In addition, this entry in familysearch.org says that the immigration was in 1855.

Wolf Vanderlinden also reports on the Internet at casebook.org under suspects / carl-feigenbaum.html that Johann Zahn not only visited his brother Anton in prison the day before the execution, but also informed the press (in Vanderlinden: "Feigenbaum's brother also told the press") that Anton Zahn did duty on the ship "Bremen" in May 1891, was a seaman there until the beginning of 1892 and then gave up the sea.

On familysearch.org there is now an entry for an Anton Zahn who was born in Germany in 1841 and who lived in the city of Syracuse in the state of New York in 1892. The exact name is "Syracuse, 12, 06, County Onondaga, New York State".

The author, who was born in 1843, found another "Anton Zahn" in Germany. Unfortunately, not all church registers in Germany are shown on familysearch.org. The first name Anton is not as common as the first name Johann or Hans. So let's assume that it is Anton Zahn from Gau-Bickelheim in Syracuse. This is perhaps supported by a married woman Zahn in Syracuse, who also comes from Rheinhessen and with whom he could have made contact.

Thus, Johann Zahn's statement is not wrong. Wolf Vanderlinden is not sure about this. But the entry found by the author of this book in the New York State Census 1892 (link on familysearch.org) does not at least prove the opposite.

Vanderlinden reports from the April 28, 1896 article in the Chicago Daily Tribune that Anton Zahn, alias Carl Feigenbaum, had been a seaman for an unknown time, possibly all his life. His lawyer Lawton states that Anton Zahn was a firefighter on the Atlantic cruisers (English liners) for many years, sometimes on the "Bremen", other times on the "White Star", sometimes on French ships and "Inman." Liners ".

Anton's brother Johann continues to tell the press the following:
"I saw and knew so little about him. As a result, I don't know where he went in the last few years. I know he was in Illinois and Wisonsin, but I don't really know - in fact". After he had chosen the profession of gardener, he was all over the west (Note by the author: Johann Zahn probably means "west of New England"). "And he traveled a lot!"

Game of Anton Zahn with names

Before it is forgotten for later, it should be noted at this point that Anton Zahn probably likes to play with people's surnames. That will become an important point later when it comes to the Ripper murders in London in 1888.

At least one can state here that his lawyer, provided he could choose him himself, is called Lawton, which contains the word "Law".

Furthermore, one of the priests who accompany him to the scaffold bears the German family name "Bruder". One can certainly argue about the symbolism here.

The second priest was called "Creeden", which is reminiscent of the Latin "credere" (to believe).

Appearance of Anton Zahn 1894 to 1896

Attorney Lawton says to Anton Zahn according to the New York Times of April 29, 1896: "I always considered him a cunning fellow, surrounded by a great deal of mystery, and his life history was never found out."

One of the US newspapers describes him as "a little, wrinkled old fellow, shabbily dressed". It sounds similar in a witness description of the man who was seen in London shortly before the murder of Annie Chapman on September 8, 1888. But that would be too little to refer Anton Zahn to London.

In the press he is described as follows:

"54 years old, 5 feet 4 inches tall, 126 pounds weight, medium complexion, black-brown hair (thin on top), narrow gray deep-set eyes, a high and heavily arched forehead and a large red nose with pimples on it.

Some points in the description fit to a certain extent with the Horrweiler-born serial killer Johann Schmitt alias Johann Otto Hoch (1855 - 1906).

The people in this area are more related to the French or Italian types. However, in northwestern Rheinhessen (and elsewhere) there are also redheads with freckles from ancient times (from the Celts, as in Ireland) and blondes who immigrated from Scandinavia.

Although it is not mentioned on the prison's entry form, drawings by Anton Zahn made during the trial indicate that he also had a mustache. In addition, a small beard could be seen on a later drawing.

Inner urge to kill women

When his legal counsel Lawton asked him head-on (for the sake of form, although it was obvious) whether he had killed Ms. Juliane Hoffman, Anton Zahn replied:

"I have for years suffered from a singular disease, which induces an all absorbing passion. This passion manifests itself in a desire to kill and mutilate the woman who falls in my way. At such times I am unable to control myself."

Wolf Vanderlinden, however, leads the lawyer Hugh Pentecost, who tried together with William Lawton to save the life of Anton Zahn. In contrast to Lawton, Pentecost said that nothing in Anton Zahn pointed to Jack the Ripper.

While the Briton Trevor Marriott goes overboard to equate Anton Zahn with the ripper, the American Wolf Vanderlinden tries exactly the opposite. He reinterprets everything so that Anton Zahn couldn't have been Jack the Ripper.

Wolf Vanderlinden even claims that Anton Zahn could not speak any English (and understood only poorly) and that his lawyer Lawton probably did not speak to him in German either. Vanderlinden thus assumes that Lawton was unable to communicate with his client Zahn.

On the other hand, Vanderlinden points to a statement by Lawton, where it is said that Anton Zahn was "crafty and very intelligent".

Of course, Lawton always addresses his clients as "Carl", because Anton Zahn lets himself be called Carl Feigenbaum (or Carl Ferdinand Feigenbaum) until the end:

"Carl, were you in London on this and that day in 1888?" Anton replied "Yes". Then he fell into a deep silence.

Carl Feigenbaum (also "Fiegenbaum" in the press) alias Anton Zahn came to court for the first time on October 26, 1894, before Judge Frederick Smyth. He was defended by the two attorneys previously mentioned, Lawton and Pentecost. The judges were Assistant District Attorney Vernon M. Davis and Stephen J. O'Hare.

Even in court he stubbornly claimed that Jacob Weibel, his friend, had murdered Juliane Hoffman. At one point he admitted in court that his real name was Zahn.

The efforts of the attorneys to have Anton Zahn declared mentally ill appeared to bear fruit on March 5, 1896, when the "Governer" of New York State requested Dr. Carlos F. Macdonald called in to examine the prisoner. On March 19, 1896, however, hopes that the execution would be averted vanished when Macdonald declared that Anton Zahn was sane.

Lawton states after the execution: "The man was a devil. The motive for the crime was his frightful desire for multilation". (Article on April 28, 1896 in The Steubenville Daily Herald)

Lawton, Anton Zahn was Jack the Ripper, received a little support from Assistant District Attorney Vernon M. Davis, who tried Feigenbaum, aka Zahn, as a judge: "If it could be proven that Feigenbaum was Jack the Ripper, then me would not that surprising." (Article in the New York Times)

Always a deep, gloomy mood

Ever since the author of this book had his own car from 1985 onwards and has hiked a few times, mostly with his parents' dog (Bernese Mountain Dog, Mittelschnauzer) from the village center of **Gau-Bickelheim** to the chapel on the Wißberg, he has it near **Burggasse**, where Even today, next to a large farm, there is still a Zahn winery, a very deep negative energy captured. However, the family there is likely to be very distantly related to the "victim". Seen in this way, the author is perhaps equally distantly related. One could almost have thought that one was scratching past a black hole that pulls everyone mentally into an unknown depth. A very frightening place, and the further you got away from the intersection on Dorfstrasse and Burggasse, the more comfortable you became. After the author saw Trevor Marriott's film for the first time in January 2015 and read the village of Gau-Bickelheim on Wolf Vanderlinden's internet site, he drove through Burggasse and the neighboring streets by car. Without knowing where the Anton Zahn senior family lived at that time within Gau-Bickelheim, something threatening could always be felt in this corner.

The author of this book only drove through **Horrweiler** once. One has the impression that the houses, which are very beautiful, but are close and high on the street, fall behind you on the street to kill you. But the place doesn't necessarily have a much different charisma than other places in Rheinhessen, perhaps because the case of Johann Schmitt alias Johann Otto Hoch has also been resolved.
In Gau-Bickelheim, however, the author always felt a great horror in the said corner of the village because there is a secret here.

However, the author also felt an eerie feeling in **Weintorstrasse** in **Mainz**, which was previously called Zuchthausstrasse. That could come from the many prisoners. Often in the corner behind the Haus zum Stein and the Lauteren-Hof you won't meet a soul, sometimes e.g. a nun or a strong craftsman. You can also feel a little shock. But this is certainly not comparable with the horror around Burggasse in Gau-Bickelheim.

As a boy at the age of 3 (1970) I was once in the 1888 house in **Pfaffen-Schwabenheim**. The Dittner couple lived there at the time. The mortar between the clinker bricks looked like vomit to me, especially in the direction of Gau-Bickelheim.

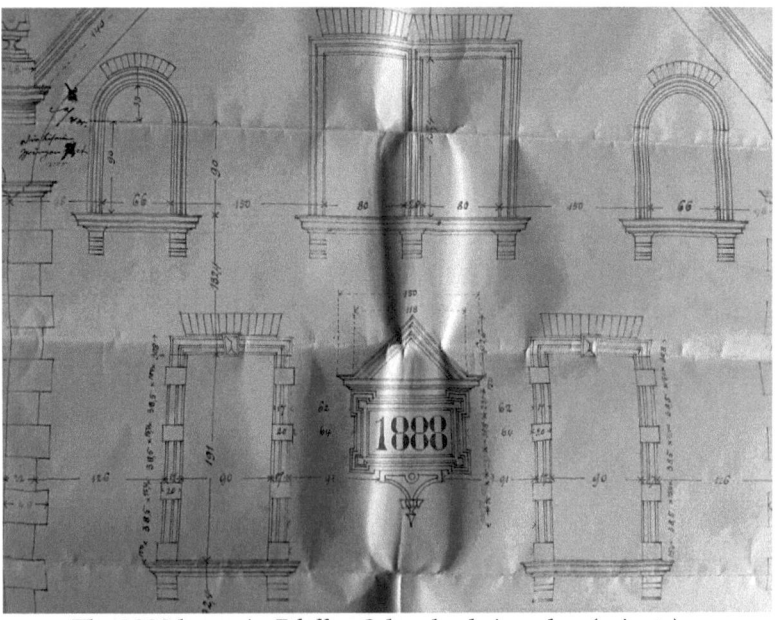

The 1888 house in Pfaffen-Schwabenheim, plan (private)

Ingelheim in 1860 – Otto Hoch was 5

Premeditated murders seem to have been quite rare in Rheinhessen in the 19th century. All the greater was the excitement when it came in Ober-Ingelheim in 1860 to two such events.

While probably the (distant) relatives of the US serial killer Johann Schmitt or Schmidt from Horrweiler alias Johann Otto Hoch were directly affected, these events could have interested Anton Zahn from Gau-Bickelheim only marginally.

After all, in one case a daughter had murdered her husband Jacob Stumpf II. (died in custody on June 25, 1862 at Marienschloß near Münzenberg) and another helper Leonhard Emmert to kill her own father Paul Daudistel.

Daudistel was first treated like a dog (handed bones to lick) in the apartment of his daughter and son-in-law and then, after he suddenly should have accepted an inheritance from his son Nicolaus Daudistel from the USA, who had long been believed dead, was "put out of the way" on June 2, 1860 early (Friday).

The monstrous thing about this case was that the daughter was sentenced to only one year in the penitentiary, and the two men received the death penalty, which, however, was not carried out. In the process, according to witnesses, the father, who was not quite dead, had called out to the daughter standing at the window while lying on the street: "Child, your father's blood cries out to you!"

Before that the mayor had still tried in a discussion with the family to bring about an improvement of the situation.

This was written in the newspaper "Rheinhessischer Beobachter". Possibly Anton Zahn read this article and again increased a little his hatred of women.

The crowd in Mainz on the day of the pronouncement of the verdict was so great that a detachment of Hessian soldiers had to hold back the 400 people in the courtroom. After questioning more than 70 witnesses from Ober-Ingelheim and investigating the murder case, the verdict was pronounced "Guilty of murder committed in conspiracy."

On April 14, 1861, at 5:30 in the morning, Jakob Stumpf was to be executed by guillotine in Mainz. This was reported by the Rheinhessischer Beobachter one day earlier. Hundreds of people then marched to Mainz at night to witness the spectacle. The accomplice Leonhard Emmert had already been pardoned to life in prison shortly before.
The executioner had already sharpened the guillotine. Respectable men, it was said, had gone to Darmstadt in an audience with the Grand Duke in this dismal matter to obtain a pardon for Jakob Stumpf II as well, which was granted.

The surname Daudistel can be proved to exist from the 17th century also in Horrweiler. There they even provide a Electoral Palatine Oberschultheiß (not mayor elected by the people) in the 18th century. A school teacher Carl Wilhelm Derscheidt, who comes from Ober-Ingelheim in the Electoral Palatinate, marries a Maria Sara Daudistel in Horrweiler in 1774.

Sometimes wealthy people move from the city to the countryside, especially since Rheinhessen is blessed with rich agriculture. So did the ancestor of the author with the surname "Bauer" from Bosenheim, who settled in Pfaffen-Schwabenheim shortly after the 30-year war. This man is married to the ancestor Sara née Gottschalk from Leiden in Holland, whose ancestors had been rope makers in Hondschoote in French Flanders. Because of the abundance of children, one brother had to leave the Dutch homeland and became a pastor in Sprendlingen (Rheinhessen).

Besides smaller dominions, Kurmainz and Kurpfalz predominated in Rheinhessen before the French Revolution. Often (but not always) the denominations Catholic and Protestant remained among themselves, and thus only certain places and families intermarried.

Thus, Gau-Algesheim and Gau-Bickelheim certainly belong in the same league on the Catholic side, and Ingelheim and Horrweiler in the same league on the Protestant side.

The second murder in Ober-Ingelheim - within a short period of time - took place on September 26, 1860, when Johann Nichtern, a 25-year-old farm laborer, stabbed to death 21-year-old Johannes Menck, who was generally considered a "good fellow." Menck was fatally wounded by Nichtern with a knife thrust behind the left ear because of the dispute about the dance order. The death sentence of the Assisengericht Mainz under the presidency of Mr. Uhler from January 19, 1861 was probably changed into a longer imprisonment. Because after searches according to ingelheim.de / stadtarchiv - details.html Johann Nichtern was born on 19 Oct. 1835 and had married on 8 May 1872. He died on 25 Dec. 1921.

Mr. Uhler was also the senior judge at Anton Zahn's court just under two and a half years later. Several judges alternate in this function from quarter to quarter.

It would have to be investigated whether Uhler in particular, in contrast to the other senior judges, treated women preferentially. The case of Elisabetha Görlipp on 21 Oct. 1863 and the case of the wife of Jacob Stumpf II on 19 Jan. 1861 seem quite strange.

Feigenbaum

The real Carl Feigenbaum (*1841; 1910 in prison)

Trevor Marriott rightly notes that he has no way of knowing what false name Anton Zahn was under before his arrest in 1894.

Nevertheless, he is desperately looking for a Carl Feigenbaum in the documents of the North German Lloyd in Bremen, where he is listed as a seaman, so that he can carry out the murders in Whitechapel in 1888 from the ships "Reiher" (engl.: Heron) and "Sperber" (engl.: Sparrowhawk) when they go ashore in the London harbor.

In his television report, Marriott points out that he was shocked when, of all things, the year 1888 can no longer be found in the form of a book with lists of crews on ships in Bremen. He suspects that the lawyer William Lawton borrowed this book from Bremen between 1894 and 1896 in 1888. But the decisive year does not necessarily have to be gone through him.

First of all, after searching for the real Carl Feigenbaum, whose name Anton Zahn uses, we come a little further when we go to the website forum.casebook.org. There various Anglo-Saxon "detectives" discuss, among other things, the entries on a sailor fig tree and a sailor tooth at the Bremen North German Lloyd (NDL).

A superintendent "Debra A" from Yorkshire in England wrote there in February 2008 that under the name "Carl Feigenbaum" he only found a blond man who was born in Demmin (Mecklenburg) in 1844. According to New York Prison Sing Sing, Anton Zahn had brown-black hair instead of blond and was born in 1840 or 1841 instead of 1844.

In addition, Anton Zahn had initially stated that he was Carl Feigenbaum from Karlsruhe, which is in Baden and not in

Mecklenburg. There are today and were actually evangelicals near Karlsruhe who are called Feigenbaum. There are a total of five entries by this blond Carl Feigenbaum, who was born in Demmin in 1844:

• Carl Feigenbaum, age 25, year of birth 1844, place of birth Demmin, place of residence Demmin, inspected on Nov. 5, 1869, ship Union, departure from Bremen, destination New York.

• Carl Feigenbaum, age 27, year of birth 1844, place of birth Demmin, place of residence Demmin, sampled on 5th Sep. 1871, ship Ohio, departure from Bremen, destination New York.

• Carl Feigenbaum, age 29, year of birth 1844, place of birth Demmen, place of residence Demmen, inspected on Feb. 21, 1873, ship Schwalbe, departure in Bremen, port of destination England (possibly place Goole).

• Carl Feigenbaum, age 29, year of birth 1844, place of birth Demmin, place of residence Demmin, sampled on March 5, 1873, ship Hanover, departure from Bremen, destination West Indies (i.e. the Caribbean).

• Carl Feigenbaum, age 29, year of birth 1844, place of birth Demmin, residence Demmin, inspected on May 20, 1873, ship Cologne, departure in Bremen, destination New York.

Debra A from Yorkshire, (where one speaks "hand" and "bus" in the English dialect instead of "hand" and "bas" as in Oxford, because that is where the Roman capital York is and one has the written language for the English developed,) writes further that in addition to the crew lists there are also registers for the sailors. In the latter, fig tree with his full name Carl Jos. Theod. Friedr. Martin Feigenbaum noted. There is also his exact date of birth, July 26, 1844, and the place of birth Demmin.

Debra A realizes that Trevor Marriott is totally wrong with his Carl Feigenbaum, which Wolf Vanderlinden confirms on the same website. Marriott had already admitted, however, that before 1892 Anton Zahn could have had another false name, i.e. not Feigenbaum.

Debra A further explains that he only found one entry for a "tooth" in the team lists, namely the one from 1872. There is a Carl Ludwig Zahn who was born in 1853 and is therefore more than ten years younger (!) than Anton Zahn is. This Carl Ludwig Zahn is also noted in the lists of desertions, where it is said that he did not board his ship after arriving in New York in 1872.

The author of this book actually finds a Carl Feigenbaum who was born in 1844 on familysearch.org. The USA Census states for 1880 that a 36 years old Charles Fergenbaum from Germany lives in Hoboken, County Hudson, State of New Jersey. Hoboken is on the Hudson River across the street from Manhattan. He is married to Annie from Austria, 24 years old, and has two daughters Rosey (2 years) and Emma (0 years). In addition, a certain Charles Wehner, 21 years old, also from Germany, lives with the family.

It also says elsewhere that a Charles born in 1844. Feigenbaum married a Kate Gartner on January 3, 1883 in Hoboken, County Hudson, New Jersey.

That could mean that Annie, his first wife, died in 1881 or 1882. We are probably looking at the sailor from Demmin, who is three years younger than Anton Zahn and, unlike Zahn, is blond.

We are lucky, and we find another Charles Feigenbaum on familysearch.

This Carl Feigenbaum was born in Germany in 1841, the same year as Anton Zahn from Gau-Bickelheim.

This fig tree, more suitable for the alias, immigrated to the USA in 1880. He is white and his relationship with the owner of the apartment in 1910 at Newark Ward 9, County Essex,

New Jersey is called "inmate". "Inmate" means prisoner, inmate, detainee or colloquially housemate. It is said that he was a widower in 1910 and 69 years old.

With extensive research, it may be possible to determine whether this man was already in jail in 1894. Because then Anton Zahn's approach would be as follows:

He looks for a person who has been sentenced to life imprisonment and takes their name.

Anton Zahn may have done it that way before.

It would, however, be a greater effort, because not only lifelong prisoners would have to be found in Rheinhessen, but elsewhere as well. In addition, they would have to be born in 1841, be about the same size, and have about the same hair and eye color.

Then you could go back to the Bremen archives for the lists of the crews.

Fig tree cursed by Jesus

The Italian director Pier Paolo Pasolini took the Bible himself as the script for his 1964 film "The 1st Gospel of Matthew". Anyone who knows the Bible inside and out will find the film almost boring in a certain way.

But some scenes are particularly highlighted that had not been given too much attention before. So also the story about the cursed fig tree.

According to the Gospel of Mark, Jesus was suddenly hungry (after leaving Bethany and before cleaning the temple). In the distance he saw a fig tree and wanted to eat its fruit. When he and his disciples got there, there were only leaves on the tree but no fruit. Then he cursed the fig tree.

One day after Jesus drove the traders from the temple in great anger, they passed the fig tree again the next morning. It was withered to the roots.

In the Gospel of Matthew, among other things, the sentence of Mark is missing: "It was not the time of the fig harvest". Everyone may think differently of this story about Jesus. In relation to Anton Zahn one could read the symbolism, the Rheinhess is convinced that he was cursed by Jesus. Hence his last alias goes well with him.

Tombstones in Pfaffen-Schwabenheim of Köth II. and IV.

190

Sketches of angles and distances

Angle in London 1888

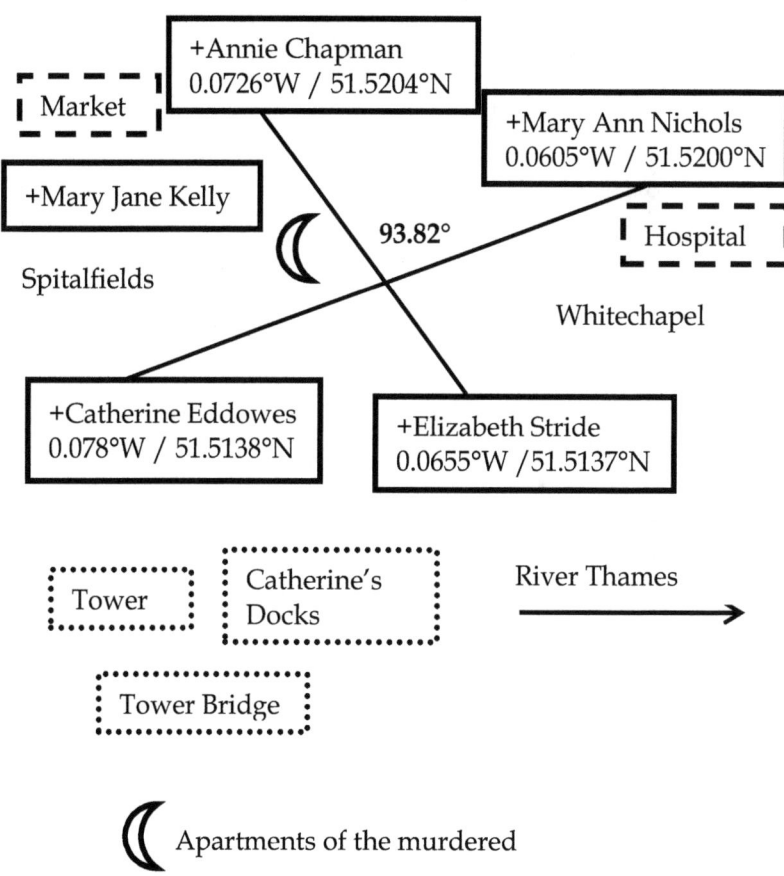

Market

+Annie Chapman
0.0726°W / 51.5204°N

+Mary Ann Nichols
0.0605°W / 51.5200°N

+Mary Jane Kelly

93.82°

Hospital

Spitalfields

Whitechapel

+Catherine Eddowes
0.078°W / 51.5138°N

+Elizabeth Stride
0.0655°W /51.5137°N

Tower

Catherine's
Docks

River Thames

Tower Bridge

Apartments of the murdered

London angle in Rheinhessen

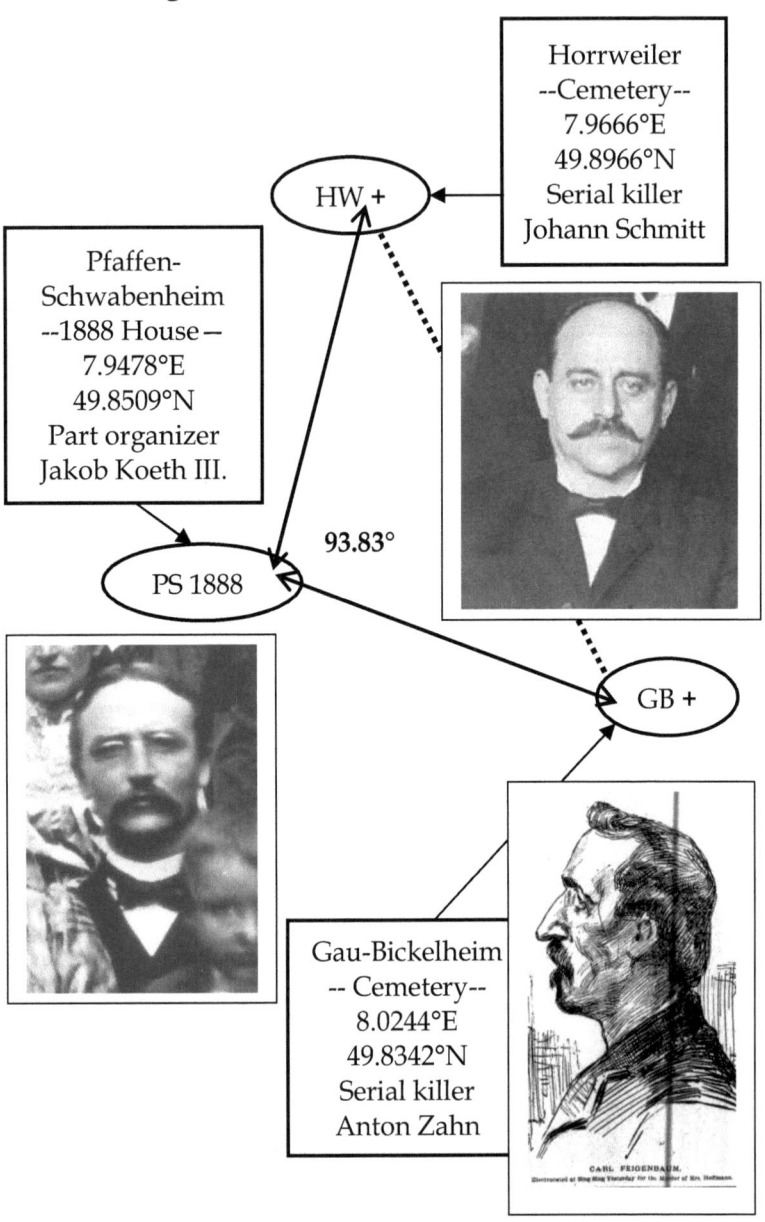

Horrweiler
--Cemetery--
7.9666°E
49.8966°N
Serial killer
Johann Schmitt

HW +

Pfaffen-
Schwabenheim
--1888 House—
7.9478°E
49.8509°N
Part organizer
Jakob Koeth III.

PS 1888

93.83°

GB +

Gau-Bickelheim
-- Cemetery--
8.0244°E
49.8342°N
Serial killer
Anton Zahn

CARL FEIGENBAUM.

Bingen to Lonsheim 1+8+8+8 km

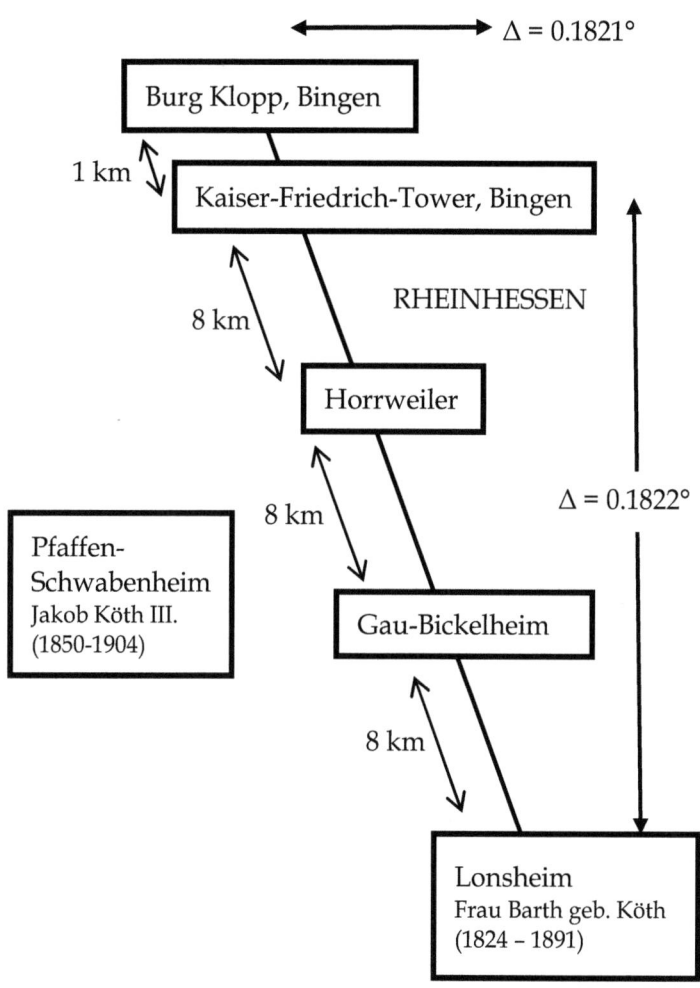

Δ = 0.1821°

Burg Klopp, Bingen

1 km

Kaiser-Friedrich-Tower, Bingen

RHEINHESSEN

8 km

Horrweiler

Δ = 0.1822°

Pfaffen-
Schwabenheim
Jakob Köth III.
(1850-1904)

8 km

Gau-Bickelheim

8 km

Lonsheim
Frau Barth geb. Köth
(1824 – 1891)

Angle between Arran, Berlin, "Carlsruhe" (ABC)

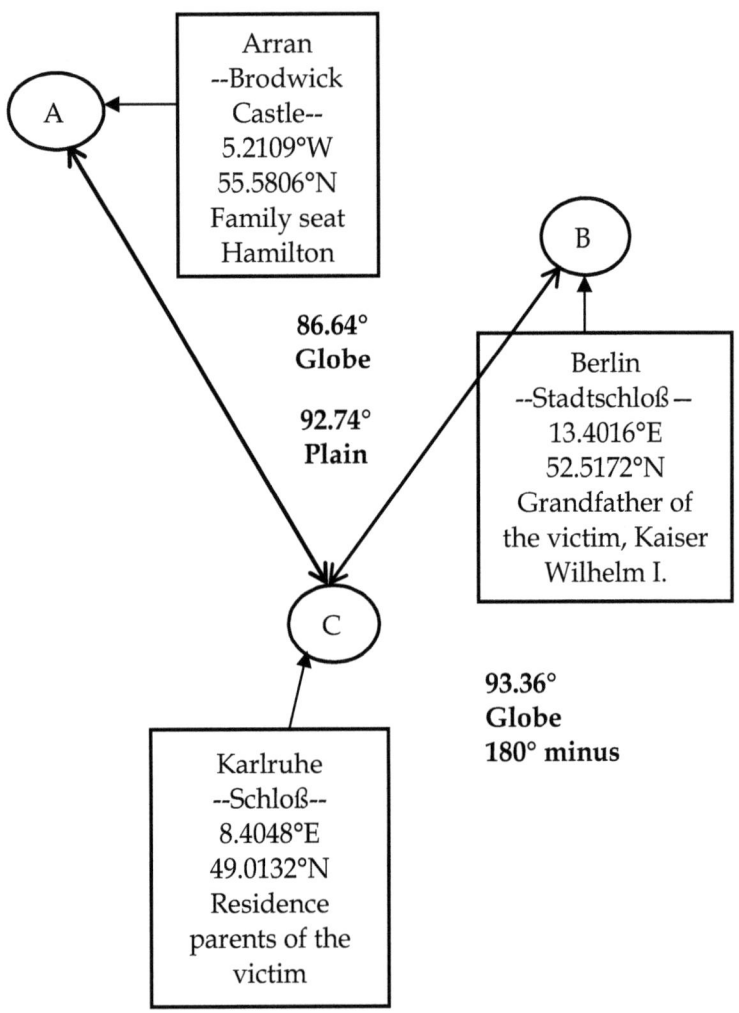

A

Arran
--Brodwick
Castle--
5.2109°W
55.5806°N
Family seat
Hamilton

B

Berlin
--Stadtschloß —
13.4016°E
52.5172°N
Grandfather of
the victim, Kaiser
Wilhelm I.

86.64°
Globe

92.74°
Plain

C

93.36°
Globe
180° minus

Karlruhe
--Schloß--
8.4048°E
49.0132°N
Residence
parents of the
victim

Extension to Stuttgart

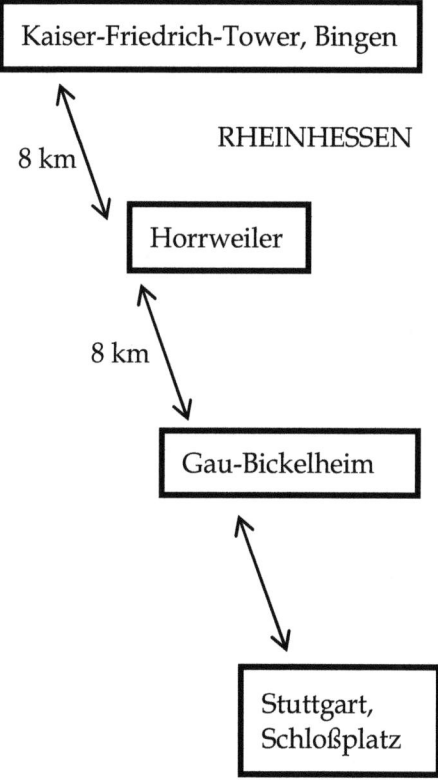

Extension to Kaiserslautern

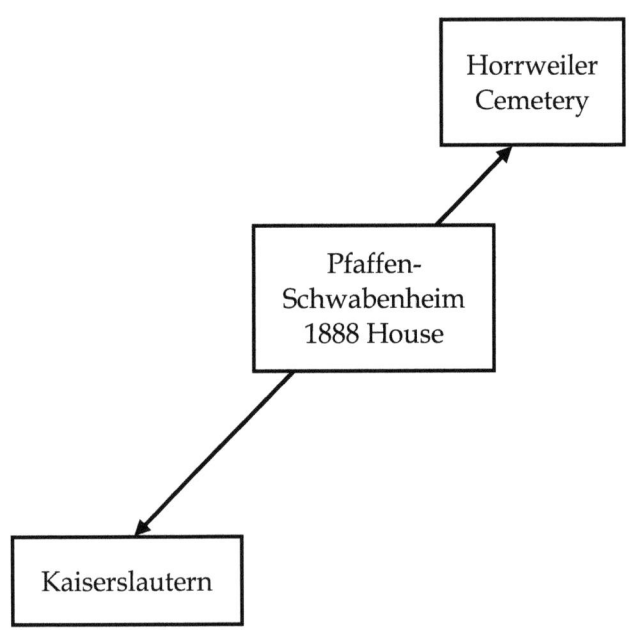

Extension to Bonn

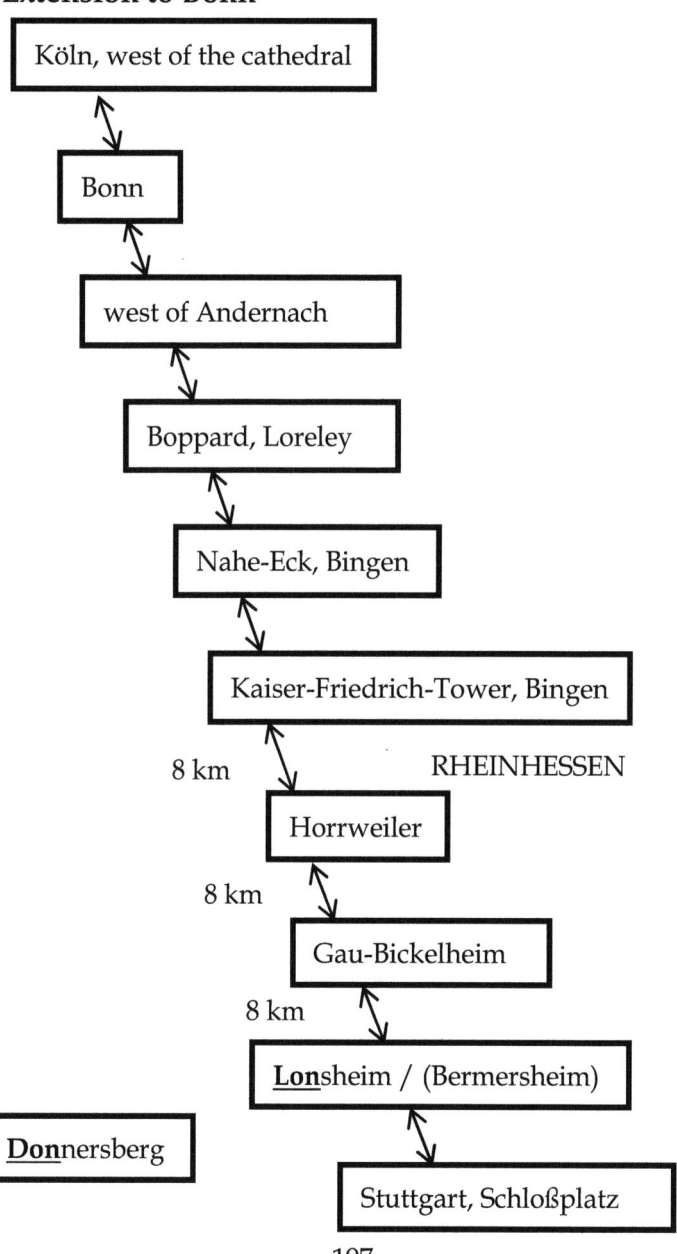

Köln, west of the cathedral

Bonn

west of Andernach

Boppard, Loreley

Nahe-Eck, Bingen

Kaiser-Friedrich-Tower, Bingen

RHEINHESSEN

8 km

Horrweiler

8 km

Gau-Bickelheim

8 km

Lonsheim / (Bermersheim)

Donnersberg

Stuttgart, Schloßplatz

197

Hanbury 29 identified from location 1888 house

In order to depict the name of Herbert von Bismarck, the street names in London are largely fixed. The positions of Buck's Row, Berner Street and Miter Square have relatively little leeway in relation to one another when it comes to the angle. Only Hanbury Street can be used to "play" extremely: from 105 ° to 49 °. The house number 29 only came about because the angle of 93.82 ° then becomes the same angle as between the two cemeteries in Horrweiler and Gau-Bickelheim and the 1888 house in Pfaffen-Schwabenheim. It is said that the murder in the back yard at 29 Hanbury Street was the riskiest because numerous tenants might have noticed. But because of the angle, it was bound to be right there. Perhaps one or more people had helped to take a closer look at the crime.

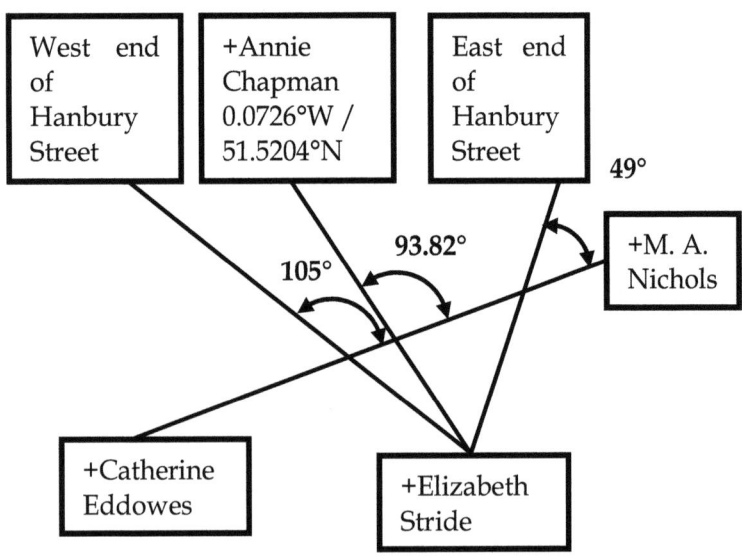

60 km to Koblenz and Frankfurt

There is an obvious connection with the grandmother of Prince Ludwig von Baden (1865-1888), Empress Augusta (1811-1890) of Saxe-Weimar-Eisenach, via the facilities in Koblenz that she commissioned.

The distance to Frankfurt is also astonishing. This could be symbolic of the coronation path between the cathedral and the town hall (Römer).

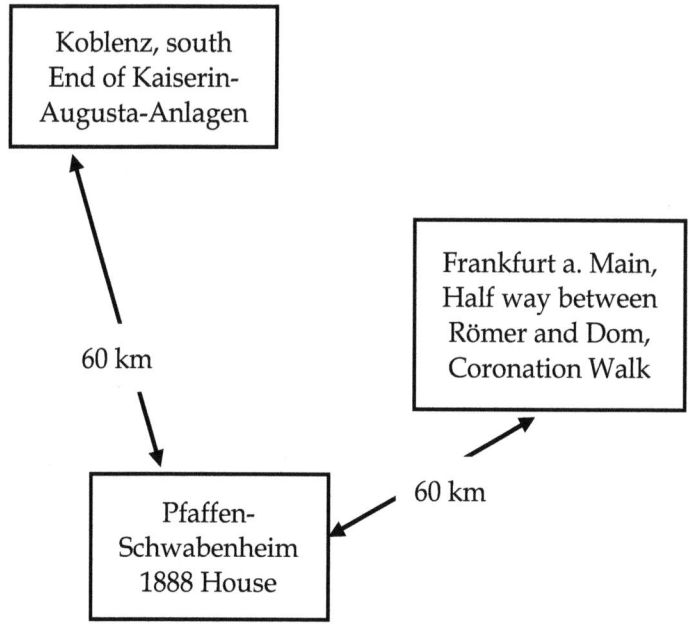

600 km to London – 6 km to 1888 house

It is probably no coincidence that the conspirators work with
the powers of ten of the number "6", namely 6 km, 60 km
and 600 km.

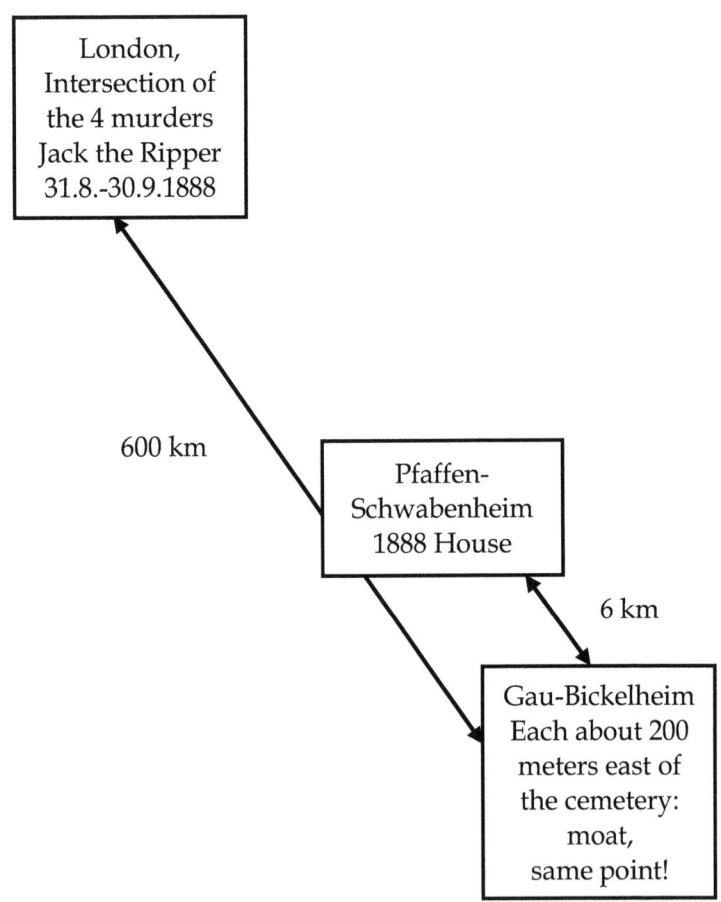

Documents about Zahn

Gau-Bickelheim, Church book, birth Anton Zahn, 17.5.1841

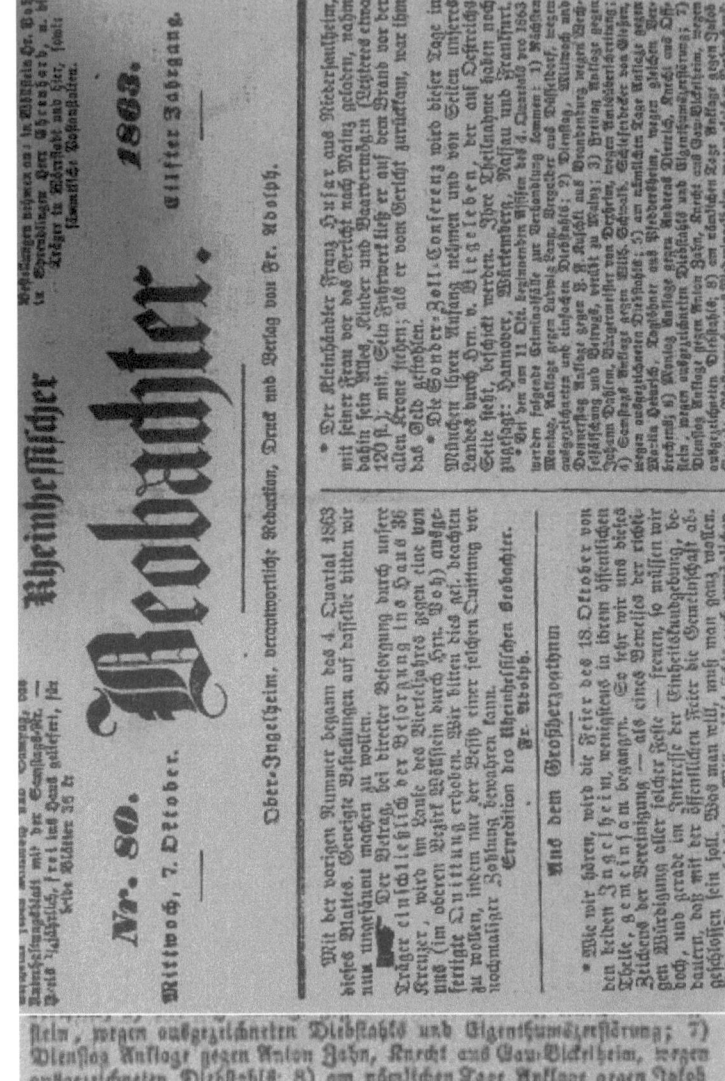

Announcement of court hearings in Mainz, in the Rheinhessischer Beobachter from October 7th, 1863, including the name "Anton Zahn, farmhand from Gau-Bickelheim"
unter: tudigit.ulb.tu-darmstadt.de

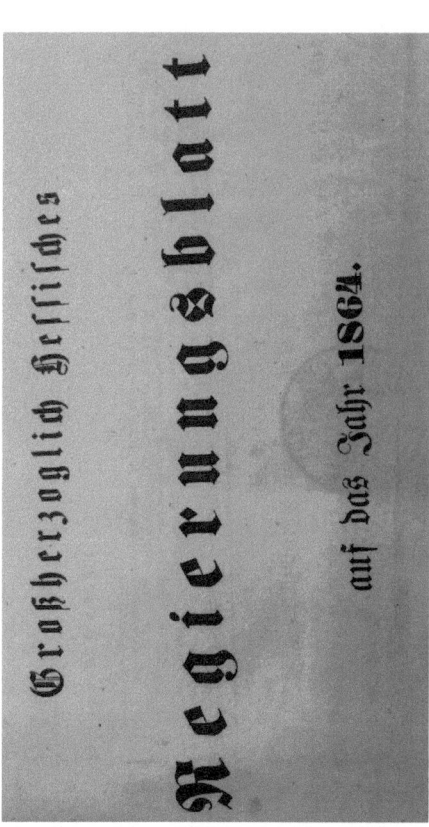

Großherzoglich Hessisches

Regierungsblatt

auf das Jahr 1864.

18) Jacob Georgi, Bürstenmacher von Nieder-Ingelheim, wegen ausgezeichneten Diebstahls, durch Urtheil vom 20. October 1863 in eine Zuchthausstrafe von 4 Jahren mit Schärfung;

19) Anton Zahn, Dienstknecht von Gau-Bickelheim, wegen ausgezeichneten Diebstahls, durch Urtheil vom 20. October 1863 in eine Zuchthausstrafe von 5 Jahren;

20) Elisabetha Görlitz, Dienstmagd aus Jacobsweiler, Königreich Bayern, wegen ausgezeichneten Diebstahls, durch Urtheil vom 21. October 1863 in eine Correctionshausstrafe von 1 Jahr 6 Monaten mit Schärfung;

Condemnation of Anton Zahn in the government gazette 1864

The elder brother Carl Zahn was sentenced in Mainz in 1846
(Mainz, Stadtarchiv am Rheinufer)

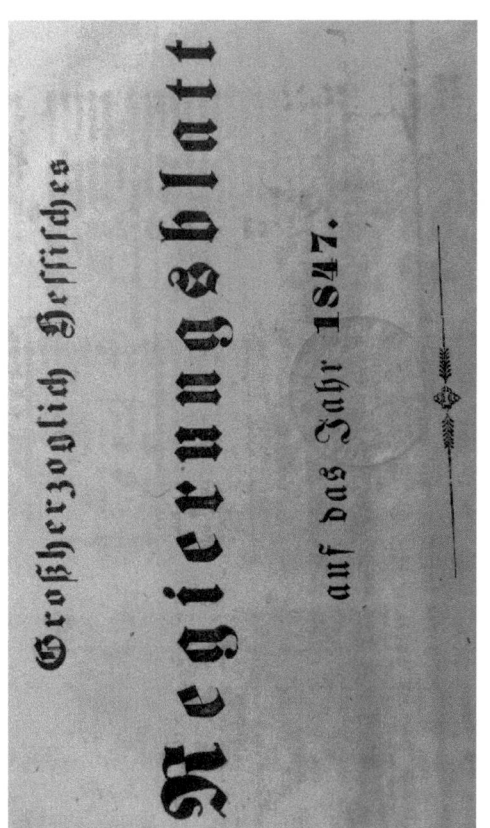

Conviction of his brother Carl Zahn in the government paper
1847

Notes on Jacob Koeth III.

Jacob Koeth's 1888 house, street front, with metal anchor, in Pfaffen-Schwabenheim, Kreuznacher Straße 31, now property of one of my female cousins (private photo 2015)

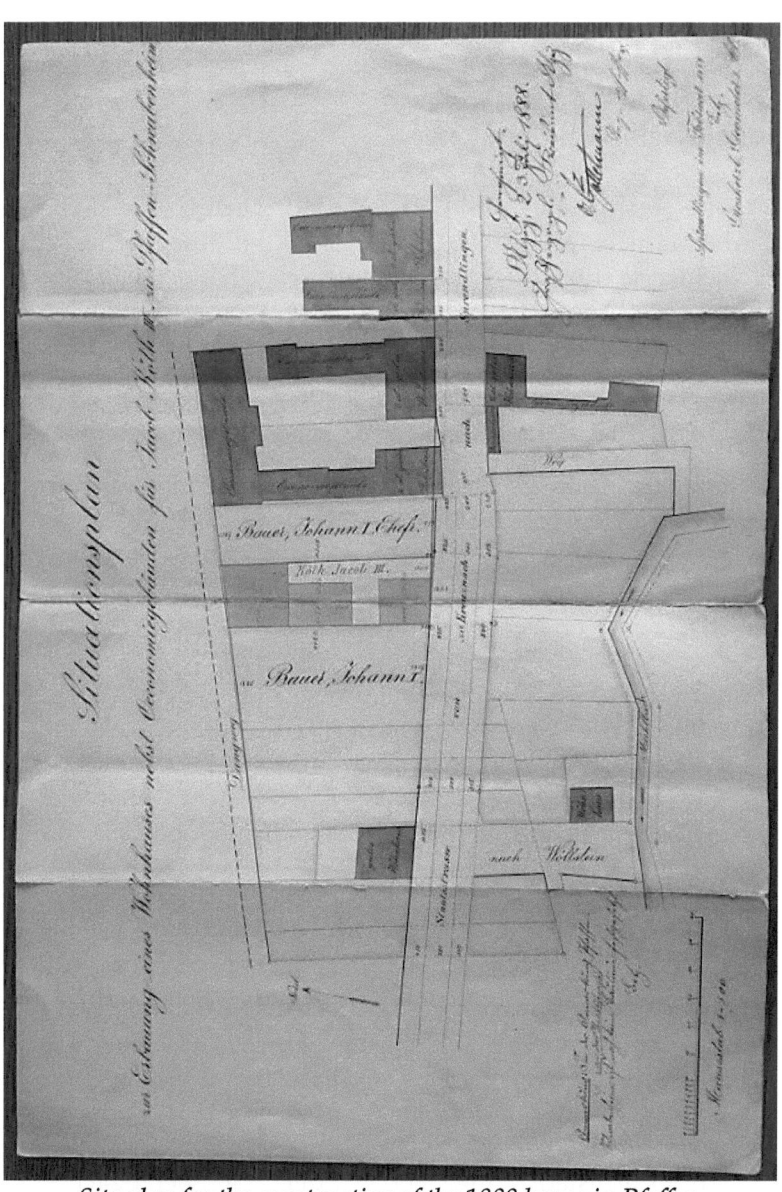

Site plan for the construction of the 1888 house in Pfaffen-Schwabenheim for Jacob Köth III. (private property)

List of references

Television and books

Götz, Hannelore und Rack, Klaus-Dieter, Hessische Abgeordnete 1820-1933, Ergänzungsband: Biographische Nachweise für die Erste Kammer der Landstände des Großherzogtums Hessen; Ergänzungen und Berichtigungen für die Zweite Kammer und den Landtag des Volksstaates Hessen, Verlag des Historischen Vereins für Hessen, Darmstadt, 1995

Hattemer, Thomas, Jack the Ripper, Verdächtiger vom Rhein, Verlag Books on Demand, Norderstedt, 2015

Hattemer, Thomas, Jack the Ripper, Deutscher vom Rhein, Verlag Books on Demand, Norderstedt, 2021

Marriott, Trevor, TV documentary "Jack the Ripper" (2011), subtitle: "The German Suspect" (The author saw the broadcast on ARTE TV in January 2015)

Newton, Michael, Die große Enzyklopädie der Serienmörder, Verlag Stocker, Graz, 2. Auflage 2005

Ruppel, Hans Georg und Groß, Birgit, Hessische Abgeordnete 1820-1933, Biographische Nachweise für die Landstände des Großherzogtums Hessen (2. Kammer) und den Landtag des Volksstaates Hessen, Verlag des Historischen Vereins für Hessen, Darmstadt, 1980

Großherzoglich Hessisches Regierungsblatt auf das Jahr 1847, Darmstadt, im Verlag der Großherzoglichen Invaliden-Anstalt

Großherzoglich Hessisches Regierungsblatt auf das Jahr 1864, Darmstadt, im Verlag der Großherzoglichen Invalidenanstalt

Original handwriting on form „Der General-Staatsprocurator am Großherzoglich Hessischen Obergerichte der Provinz Rheinhessen" 1846

Original handwriting on form „Der General-Staatsprocurator am Großherzoglich Hessischen Obergerichte der Provinz Rheinhessen" 1863 (Oktober verschollen?)

Church books of the Catholic parish Gau-Bickelheim

Chronik der Deutschen, Weltbild Verlag, Dortmund, 1983

Faßbinder, Pfarrkirche St. Martin Gau-Bickelheim, 2003

Huber, Wilhelm, Das Mainz-Lexikon, Verlag Hermann Schmidt, Mainz, 2002

Jürgensmeier, Friedhelm, Das Bistum Mainz, 2. Auflage 1989, Verlag Josef Knecht, Frankfurt am Main

Pierer's Universal-Lexikon, Band 2, Altenburg 1857

Scheel, Heinrich, Die Mainzer Republik, 2 Bände, 1981, VEB-Verlag Ost-Berlin

Internet

Google Maps

Website www.familysearch.org on family research in Germany, Great Britain and the USA (accessed in 2015)

Dan Norder, Wolf Vanderlinden, Alan Sharp: „Ripper Notes: The Legend Continues", unter "Google Books" (Read 2020)

Website for the bi-weekly newspaper „Rheinhessischer Beobachter" (Jahrgänge 1856 bis 1865 und 1873) auf Website tudigit.ulb.tu-darmstadt.de (Read Mai 2015)

Wikipedia (german) „Herbert von Bismarck (1849-1904)" (Read: 15.07.2020). Cited therein as sources:

- Walter Bußmann (Hrsg. und Einl.): Herbert Graf von Bismarck: Aus seiner politischen Privatkorrespondenz. (= Deutsche Geschichtsquellen des 19. und 20. Jahrhunderts. Band 44) Vandenhoeck & Ruprecht, Göttingen 1964.
- Winfried Baumgart (Hrsg. und Bearb.): Herbert Graf von Bismarck: Erinnerungen und Aufzeichnungen 1871–1895. Ferdinand Schöningh, Paderborn 2015; ISBN 978-3-506-78263-2.
- Eberhard von Vietsch: Bismarck, Nikolaus Heinrich Ferdinand Herbert Graf von, Fürst von. In: Neue Deutsche Biographie (NDB). Band 2, Duncker & Humblot, Berlin 1955, ISBN 3-428-00183-4, S. 268 (Digitalisat).
- Louis Leo Snyder: Political Implications of Herbert von Bismarck's Marital Affairs, 1881, 1892. In: The Journal of Modern History 36/2 (Juni 1964), S. 155–169.
- Literatur von und über Herbert von Bismarck im Katalog der Deutschen Nationalbibliothek
- Fürst von Bismarck-Schönhausen, Herbert in der Datenbank der Reichstagsabgeordneten

- Biografie von Herbert Graf-Comte Fürst Bismarck-Schoenhausen. In: Heinrich Best: Datenbank der Abgeordneten der Reichstage des Kaiserreichs 1867/71 bis 1918 (Biorab – Kaiserreich)

Wikipedia (german) „Ludwig Wilhelm von Baden (1865–1888)" (Read: 14.07.2020). Cited therein as sources:

- Ludwig Wilhelm von Baden (1865–1888) im Stadtwiki Karlsruhe
- Kurzbiographie (https://www2.landesarchiv-bw.de/ofs21/olf/einfueh.php? bestand=11214#_2)
- Wolf Ernst Hugo Emil Graf von Baudissin: Aus meiner Dienstzeit. Digitalisat
- (http://www.karlheinz-everts.de/Texte/Dienstzeit.htm) Beschreibung der Grabkapelle (http://www.grabkapelle-karlsruhe.de/erlebnisgrapkapelle/grabkapelle/)
- Warter Höhe. (http://www.warterhoehe.de/) Abgerufen am 1. Februar 2017.

Wikipedia (german) „Wolf Ernst Hugo Emil Graf von Baudissin" (Read: 14.07.2020). Cited therein as sources:

- geneanet
- Harry von Rège: "Offizier-Stammliste des Infanterie-Regiments Nr. 76"; 1902, Nummer 173, Seite 135/136
- Literatur von und über Wolf Ernst Hugo Emil von Baudissin im Katalog der Deutschen Nationalbibliothek
- Werke von Wolf Ernst Hugo Emil von Baudissin im Projekt Gutenberg-DE
- Freiherr von Schlicht (private Website von Karlheinz Everts)
- Spemanns goldenes Buch der Sitte ediert von Wolf Ernst Hugo und Eva von Baudissin im Volltext auf zeno.org

Wikipedia (german) „William Hamilton, 12. Duke of Hamilton" (Read: 18.07.2020). Cited therein as sources:

- William Alexander Louis Stephen Douglas-Hamilton, 12th Duke of Hamilton auf thepeerage.com, abgerufen am 10. September 2016.

Wikipedia (engl.) „William Douglas-Hamilton, 12th Duke of Hamilton" (Read: 20.07.2020). Cited therein as sources:

- Cokayne, G.E.; Vicary Gibbs, H.A. Doubleday, Geoffrey H. White, Duncan Warrand and Lord Howard de Walden, editors. The Complete Peerage of England, Scotland, Ireland, Great Britain and the United Kingdom, Extant, Extinct or Dormant, new ed. 13 volumes in 14. 1910–1959. Reprint in 6 volumes, Gloucester, U.K.: Alan Sutton Publishing, 2000.
- Regiments.org
- Hansard 1803–2005: contributions in Parliament by the Duke of Hamilton

Wikipedia (engl.) „Lady Mary Victoria Douglas-Hamilton" (Read: 21.07.2020). Cited therein as sources:

- "Person Page 10128". Thepeerage.com. Retrieved 27 February 2012.
- Anne Edwards, The Grimaldis of Monaco, 1992

Wikipedia (engl.) „William Hamilton, 11th Duke of Hamilton" (Read: 20.07.2020). Cited therein as sources:

- "Douglas, William Alexander Anthony Archibald" . Dictionary of National Biography. London: Smith, Elder & Co. 1885–1900.
- Doyle, J.E. (1886). Abercon-Fortescue. The Official Baronage of England: Showing the Succession, Dignities, and Offices of Every Peer from 1066 to 1885, with Sixteen Hundred Illustrations (in Spanish). Longmans, Green, and Company. p. 217. Retrieved 30 April 2019.
- Chancellor, E. Beresford (1908). The Private Palaces of London Past and Present. London: Kegan Paul, Trench, Trübner & Co Ltd. pp. 366–367. Retrieved 30 June 2015.

- Hansard 1803–2005: contributions in Parliament by the Duke of Hamilton
- William, 11th Duke of Hamilton: Hamilton Palace

Wikipedia (engl.) „Tasziló Festetics" (Read: 18.07.2020). Cited therein as sources:

- ISNI: 0000 0004 4772 3708
- VIAF: 315523564
- WorldCat Identities: viaf-315523564

Wikipedia (engl.) „Princess Marie Amelie of Baden" (Read: 18.07.2020). Cited therein as sources:

- de Saint-Amand, Imbert (1900). Napoleon III at the Height of His Power. Charles Scribner and Sons. p. 1.
- Dod, Charles Roger (1855). Peerage, Baronetage, and Knightage, Volume 15. Gilbert and Rivington.
- "English Wives of Foreign Nobleman". The Lady's Realm. Hutchinson and Co. 15. 1904.
- Leigh, Wendy (2008). True Grace: The Life and Times of an American Princess. St. Martin's Griffin. ISBN 978-0312381943.
- Lodge, Edmund (1872). The Peerage and Baronetage of the British Empire. Hurst and Blackett.
- Loliée, Frédéric; O'Donnell, Bryan (1910). The Gilded Beauties of the Second Empire. Brentano's.
- Mansel, Philip (2003). Paris Between Empires: Monarchy and Revolution 1814-1852. St. Martin's Press. p. 544. ISBN 0312308574.
- Martin, Frederick (1866). The Statesman's Year-Book. Macmillan and Co.
- Nichols Barker, Nancy (2011). Distaff Diplomacy: The Empress Eugénie and the Foreign Policy of the Second Empire. University of Texas Press. ISBN 978-0292735927.
- Ridley, Jane (2013). The Heir Apparent: A Life of Edward VII, the Playboy Prince. Random House. ISBN 978-1400062553.
- Sanders, L.C. (2004). "Hamilton, William Alexander Anthony Archibald Douglas-, eleventh duke of Hamilton and eighth

duke of Brandon (1811–1863)". Oxford Dictionary of National Biography (online ed.). Oxford University Press. doi:10.1093/ref:odnb/7939. (Subscription or UK public library membership required.)

- Württemberg, Sophie of (1989). A Stranger in The Hague: The Letters of Queen Sophie of the Netherlands to Lady Malet, 1842–1877. Duke University Press. ISBN 0822308754.

Wikipedia (german) „Marie Amelie von Baden" (Read: 18.07.2020). Cited therein as sources:

- Marie Amelie Elisabeth Karoline Prinzessin von Baden auf thepeerage.com, Abruf 11.09.2016
- Stammbaum des Hauses Baden (englisch)
- Gemälde im Schloss Mannheim
- Herzogin von Hamilton – Nachruf. In: Freie Presse, 25. Oktober 1888, S. 5 (Online bei ANNO)

Wikipedia (german) „Hamilton Palace" (Read: 20.07.2020). Cited therein as sources:

- www.slleisureandculture.co.uk
- Bruce Royan: Der virtuelle Hamilton Palast: Aufbau einer digitalen Ressource für Lokal- und Familiengeschichte (PDF; 595 kB)
- Hamilton Palace: Eine virtuelle Rekonstruktion (englisch)

Wikipedia (german) „Clan Douglas" (Read: 20.07.2020). Cited therein as sources:

- Sir William Fraser (1816-1898): The Douglas book (1885) – Internet Archive
- Ernst Heinrich Knesche: Deutsche Grafenhaeuser der Gegenwart. In heraldischer, historischer und genealogischer Beziehung. Band 3: A-Z. Weigel, Leipzig 1854, S.84
- H. Maxwell: A History of the House of Douglas, 1902 (Digitalsat auf Archive.org; englisch)

Wikipedia (german) „Paul von Hatzfeldt" (Read Juli 2020),
Cited therein as sources:

- Helmut Hirsch: Sophie von Hatzfeldt: in Selbstzeugnissen usw., 1981
- Otto Renkhoff, Nassauische Biographie, usw. 1992
- zit. nach Franz-Eugen Volz: Paul Graf von Hatzfeldt-Wildenburg. In: Lebensbilder aus dem Kreis Altenkirchen. Altenkirchen, 1975.
- Aus der Zeit des Deutsch-Französischen Krieges 1870/71 sind seine Kriegsbriefe erhalten und von seiner Ehefrau in Buchform herausgegeben worden: Graf Paul Hatzfeldt: Hatzfelds Briefe. Briefe des Grafen Paul Hatzfeldt (ehemaliger deutscher Botschafter in London, Madrid und Konstantinopel, preußischer Staatsminister) an seine Frau. Geschrieben vom Hauptquartier König Wilhelms 1870–71. Verlag Heinrich Schmidt & Carl Günther, Leipzig 1907.
- Botschafter Paul Graf von Hatzfeldt, Nachgelassene Papiere 1838–1901, Hrsg. Gerhard Ebel und Michael Behnen. 2 Bde., Boppard 1976.
- Vera Niehus: Ein ‚ambassadeur idéal', jedoch „den Anstrengungen des ministeriellen Dienstes nicht gewachsen": Paul von Hatzfeldt als außenpolitischer Mitarbeiter Bismarcks. In: Lothar Gall, Ulrich Lappenküper (Hrsg.): Bismarcks Mitarbeiter. Schöningh, Paderborn 2009, ISBN 978-3-506-76591-8.
- Franz-Eugen Volz: Paul Graf von Hatzfeldt-Wildenburg. In: Lebensbilder aus dem Kreis Altenkirchen. Altenkirchen, 1975.
- Hans Philippi: Hatzfeldt-Wildenburg, Paul Graf von. In: Neue Deutsche Biographie (NDB). Band 8, Duncker & Humblot, Berlin 1969, ISBN 3-428-00189-3, S. 65–67 (Digitalisat).

Wikipedia (german) „Kuno zu Rantzau (Diplomat)" (Read Juli 2020). Cited therein as sources:

- Bernhard Ebneth: Rantzau. In: Neue Deutsche Biographie (NDB), Band 21, Duncker & Humblot, Berlin 2003, S. 148 (Digitalsat), Familienartikel

Wikipedia (german) „Heinrich Adalbert zu Rantzau" (Read Juli 2020). Cited therein as sources, among others:

- Ernst von Mirbach, Soldatisches Führertum, Band 10, Hanseatisches Verlagsanstalt, Hamburg, ca. 1942, S. 330-332, Nr. 2345

Wikipedia (german) „Georg von Preußen" (Read März 2021). Cited therein as sources:

- Marie von Olfers: Georg Prinz von Preußen. Ein Nachruf, In: Hohenzollernjahrbuch, 6. Jg. 1902. Anhang. S. I-IV.
- Ernst von Mirbach: Prinz Friedrich von Preußen. Ein Wegbereiter der Romantik am Rhein. Böhlau-Verlag, 2006

Wikipedia (german) „Albrecht von Stosch" (Read Juli 2020). Cited therein as sources:

- Hermann von Petersdorff: Stosch, Albrecht von. In: Allgemeine Deutsche Biographie (ADB). Band 54, Duncker & Humblot, Leipzig 1908, S. 576–607.
- Kurt von Priesdorff: Soldatisches Führertum. Band 8, Hanseatische Verlagsanstalt Hamburg, o. O. [Hamburg], o. J. [1941], DNB 367632837, S. 307–318, Nr. 2618.
- Alfred von Tirpitz: Erinnerungen. Gekürzte Volksausgabe. Hase & Koehler Verlag, Leipzig 1919.
- Ernst Schröder: Albrecht von Stosch, der General-Admiral Kaiser Wilhelms I. Eine Biographie. Ebering, Berlin 1939.
- Genealogisches Handbuch des Adels. Adelige Häuser B Band XVIII, S. 462, Band 95 der Gesamtreihe. C. A. Starke, Limburg (Lahn) 1989.
- Gerd Fesser: General – Admiral – Kanzlerkandidat. In: Schiff Classic, Magazin für Schifffahrts- und Marinegeschichte e.V. der DGSM, Ausgabe: 3/2020, S. 36–39.

- Acta Borussica Band 6/I (1867–1878)
- Acta Borussica Band 6/II (1867–1878)
- Acta Borussica Band 7 (1879–1890) (PDF; 2,8 MB)
- Acta Borussica Band 8/I (1890–1900) (PDF; 2,7 MB)
- Acta Borussica Band 8/II (1890–1900) (PDF; 2,2 MB)
- 'Stosch, Albrecht von'. In: Meyers. 6. Auflage. Band 19, S. 70–71.
- Gothaisches Genealogisches Taschenbuch der Briefadeligen Häuser. 1907. Erster Jahrgang, Justus Perthes, Gotha 1906, S. 754.

Wikipedia (german) „Heinrich Eduard von Lade" (Read: 14.07.2020). Cited therein as sources:

- Franz Jahn, Eduard Lucas, Johann Georg Conrad Oberdieck: Illustrirtes Handbuch der Obstkunde (http://pomologie.ub.tuberlin. de/Ill__Handb__der_Obstkunde/body_ill__handb__der_ob stkunde.html) in 9 Bänden und einigen Zusatzbänden, 1859–1883, das pomologische Standardwerk des 19. Jahrhunderts.
- Wilhelm Oncken: Freiherr Eduard von Lade und sein Landhaus am Rhein, Berlin 1904. (Digitalisat (http://digital.ub.uniduesseldorf. de/content/titleinfo/1716917)).
- Paul Claus: Geisenheimer Erinnerungen. (1817–1972). Eduard von Lade und die Lehr- und Forschungsanstalt (= Beiträge zur Kultur und Geschichte der Stadt Geisenheim. Bd. 8, ZDB-ID 2240236-6). Förderkreis Kulturdenkmäler
- Geisenheim, Geisenheim 2005.
- Helmut Hans Dittrich: Lade, Eduard Freiherr von. In: Neue Deutsche Biographie (NDB). Band 13, Duncker & Humblot, Berlin 1982, ISBN 3-428-00194-X, S. 382 f. (Digitalisat).

m.faz.net, Frankfurter Allgemeine Zeitung im Internet, Rubrik: Region und Hessen. Artikel: Heinrich Eduard von Lade, Anführer der Rheingauer Wutbürger. Von: Oliver Bock, Geisenheim, updated on 16.02.2017. (Read: 14.07.2020)

„Preußische Rheinregulierung bei Geisenheim". In: KuLaDig. Kultur.Landschaft.Digital. URL: https://www.kuladig.de/Objektansicht/KLD-274543" (Read: 28.11.2020)

www.hs-geisenheim.de (Read: 28.12.2020)
Website of: Hochschule Geisenheim University /Hochschule/Profil/Geschichte/ und /Hochschule/ Profil/Zahlen und Fakten/Entwicklung seit 1872/

Wikipedia (german) „Ludwig Bamberger" (Read Juli 2020). Numerous sources are cited therein, including:

- Fritz Specht, Paul Schwabe: Die Reichstagswahlen von 1867 bis 1903. Eine Statistik der Reichstagswahlen nebst den Programmen der Parteien und einem Verzeichnis der gewählten Abgeordneten. 2. Auflage. Verlag Carl Heymann, Berlin 1904

Zu den Wahlkreisen und Abstimmungsergebnissen s.u. „zhsf.gesis.org" (Read März 2021)

Wikipedia (german) „Kaiserliche Admiralität" (Read: 28.12.2020). Cited therein as a source:

- Walther Hubatsch: Der Admiralstab und die obersten Marinebehörden in Deutschland, 1848-1945, Frankfurt a.M.: Bernard & Gaefe, 1958

Wikipedia (german) „Preußische Landesaufnahme (Behörde)" (Read: 28.12.2020). Cited therein as a source:

- Oskar Albrecht: Beiträge zum militärischen Vermessungs- und Kartenwesen und zur Militärgeographie in Preußen (1803-1921), Amt für Geoinformationswesen der Bundeswehr, Schriftenreihe, Heft 1, Euskirchen, 2004

Wikipedia (german) „Großer Generalstab" (Read: 28.12.2020). Cited therein as sources:

- Walter Görlitz: Geschichte des deutschen Generalstabes von 1650-1945, Eltville 1997, ISBN 3-86047-918-0
- Christian E.O. Millotat: Das preussisch-deutsche Generalstabsystem: Wurzeln – Entwicklung – Fortwirken, vdf Hochschulverlag, Zürich, 2000, ISBN 3-7281-2749-3
- Lukas Grawe: Feindaufklärung im preußisch-deutschen Generalstab vor 1914, Militärgeschichte, Zeitschrift für historische Bildung 4/2013 S.10-13

Wikipedia (german) „Markgrafschaft Baden-Baden" (Read 29.11.2020). Source used i.a.

- Armin Kohnle: Kleine Geschichte der Markgrafschaft Baden, Verlag G. Braun, Karlsruhe, 2007, ISBN 978-3-7650-8346-4

Wikipedia (german) „Charles_Woodcock" (Read: 12.12.2020). Cited therein as sources:

- Hauptstaatsarchiv Stuttgart, E 75 (Württembergische Gesandtschaft in München) Bü 6 (Presseerörterungen betr. den Freiherrn von Woodcock-Savage, 1888)
- Übersendung der dem Gesandten in München von dem Bayerischen Major z.D. Freiherr von der Heydte übergebenen Papiere aus dem Nachlass des ehemaligen Bankdirektors L. Colin, betr. den Amerikaner Woodcock-Savage. Hauptstaatsarchiv Stuttgart, E 55
- Roots: Charles Burger Woodcock
- Bernd-Ulrich Hergemöller: Mann für Mann – Biographisches Lexikon zur Geschichte von Freundesliebe und mannmännlicher Sexualität im deutschen Sprachraum. Hamburg 1998.
- Jürgen Honeck: Der Liebhaber des Königs. Skandal am württembergischen Hof. Mühlacker Irdning/Steiermark 2012. ISBN 9783798704084.

- Jonathan Ned Katz: Americans in Württemberg Scandal. OutHistory in 4 Teilen.
- Paul Sauer: Regent mit mildem Zepter. König Karl von Württemberg. DVA, Stuttgart 1999. ISBN 3-421-05181-X. (Zu Woodcock: S. 229ff)
- Charles Savage: A Lady in Waiting: Being extracts from the diary of Julie de Chesnil, sometime lady-in-waiting to her Majesty, Queen Marie Antoinette New York: D. Appleton & Company 1906.
- Geoffrey Dayton Smith: American Fiction, 1901-1925: A Bibliography (Cambridge University Press, 1997) no. W-847.

Wikipedia (german) „Karl_(Württemberg)" (Read: 12.12.2020). Cited therein as sources:

- Friedrich Freiherr Hiller von Gaertringen: Karl, König von Württemberg. In: Neue Deutsche Biographie (NDB). Band 11, Duncker & Humblot, Berlin 1977, ISBN 3-428-00192-3, S. 269 f. (Digitalisat).
- Jürgen Honeck: Drei württembergische Könige. Ihre Persönlichkeit im Spiegel von Politik, Macht und Liebe, Stieglitz, Mühlacker und Irdning/Steiermark 2008, ISBN 978-3-7987-0393-3.
- Hubert Krins: Könige und Königinnen von Württemberg. Lindenberg 2007 (3. Auflage). ISBN 978-3-89870-024-5.
- Ulrike Landfester, Friderike Loos (Hrsg.): Lieber Kronprinz! Liebe Freundin! Briefwechsel zwischen Bettine von Arnim und Karl von Württemberg. Mit einem Anhang: Briefwechsel zwischen Bettine von Arnim und Julius von Hardegg. Manutius, Heidelberg 1998, ISBN 3-925678-82-4.
- Sönke Lorenz, Dieter Mertens, Volker Press (Hrsg.): Das Haus Württemberg. Ein biographisches Lexikon. Kohlhammer, Stuttgart 1997, ISBN 3-17-013605-4, S. 319–323.
- Sophie Dorothee Podewils (Hrsg.): Traum der Jugend goldner Stern. Aus den Aufzeichnungen der Königin Olga von Württemberg [Aus dem französischen Manuskript übersetzt von Sophie Dorothee Gräfin Podewils]. Neske, Pfullingen 1955.

- Paul Sauer: Regent mit mildem Zepter. König Karl von Württemberg. DVA, Stuttgart 1999. ISBN 3-421-05181-X.
- Paul Friedrich von Stälin: Karl I. Friedrich Alexander, König von Württemberg. In: Allgemeine Deutsche Biographie (ADB). Band 51, Duncker & Humblot, Leipzig 1906, S. 57–65.
- Constantin von Wurzbach: Württemberg, Karl Friedrich Alexander König von. In: Biographisches Lexikon des Kaiserthums Oesterreich. 58. Theil. Kaiserlich-königliche Hof- und Staatsdruckerei, Wien 1889, S. 244 (Digitalisat).
- Jürgen Honeck: Der Liebhaber des Königs. Skandal am württembergischen Hof, Stieglitz, Mühlacker und Irdning/Steiermark 2012, ISBN 978-3-7987-0408-4.
- Werke von und über Karl in der Deutschen Digitalen Bibliothek
- Gerhard Fritz: König Karl von Württemberg (1823-1891), publiziert am 19. April 2018 in: Stadtarchiv Stuttgart: Stadtlexikon Stuttgart

Wikipedia (engl.) „Johann Otto Hoch" (Read: 2015 and 12.12.2020). Cited therein as sources:

- Lydersen, Kari (31 Oct 2006). "Infamous Piece of Chicago History Goes on the Block". Washington Post. Retrieved 24 April 2013.
- Schutzer, A. I. (October 1964). "The Lady-killer". American Heritage. Retrieved 24 April 2013.
- Hoch v. People, 76 N.E. 356, 357 (Supreme Court of Illinois 20 December 1905).
- "Remarkable Career of Bluebeard Hoch". Perrysville Journal (Ohio). 24 Feb 1905. Retrieved 24 April 2013.
- Clinton Mirror Feb 25, 1905
- Fluharty, Linda Cunningham (2009). "Caroline Miller Hoch Huff: Victim of a Serial Killer". The WVGenWeb Project: West Virginia Genealogy. Retrieved 24 April 2013.
- "Re: Mary Schulte missing after 1900?". GenForum. Genealogy.com. 6 December 2008. Retrieved 24 April 2013.
- San Francisco Calls January 11 and 22, February 2 and 10, 1905

Wikipedia (engl.) „Carl Feigenbaum" (Read: 21.01.2021). Cited therein as sources (mostly in Spanish):

- Wolf Vanderlinden, Carl Ferdinand Feigenbaum: An old suspect resurfaces, artículo reproducido en el sitio web Casebook Jack the Ripper y en la revista Ripper Notes n° 28, marzo 2008.
- William Lawton, artículo publicado en el New York Times el 29 de abril de 1896, y reproducido por el sitio web "Casebook Jack the Ripper".
- Trevor Marriott, Jack the Ripper: The 21st Century Investigation, Editorial John Blake Publishing, Londres, Inglaterra (2007), págs. 285-354.
- "Jack the Ripper": A 21st Century Investigation, sitio digital de Trevor Marriott.
- Trevor Marriott, Jack the Ripper: The 21st Century Investigation, obra citada, págs. 293-296; 312-315
- Gabriel Pombo, Jack el Destripador: La leyenda continúa, Montevideo, Uruguay (2010), págs. 73.
- Gabriel Pombo, Jack el Destripador: La leyenda continúa (reedición ampliada, en google libros), editorial Torre del Vigía, Montevideo, 2015, ISBN 978 9974 99 868 1, pág 55-56.
- Arquímedes González Torres, La muerte de acuario, Editorial Distribuidora Cultural, Managua, Nicaragua (2005).

Wolf Vanderlinden „Carl Ferdinand Feigenbaum: An Old Suspect Resurfaces" at Website www.casebook.org/suspects/carl-feigenbaum.html (Read 23.1.2015) Cited as sources there:

- The Ann Arbor Register, 30 April 1896 (Anmerkung zu „Ganbickelheim, Alzei": Wolf Vanderlinden ist unklar, warum „Hesse-Darmstadt" dasteht, weil heute in Rheinland-Pfalz. / Bei anderer Fußnote wundert sich Vanderlinden, daß die Schwester von Anton Zahn, Magdalena [Strohband] 55 Meilen nördlich von Karlsruhe wohnt.)
- The Fort Wayne News, 27.4.1896
- John Blake Publishing Inc. 2007

- The New York Times, 1.9.1895 / 29.4.1896
- The Chicago Daily Tribune, 2.9.1894 / 28.4.1896
- The Brooklyn Eagle, 30.4.1891 / 1.9.1894
- The Washington Post, 28.4.1896
- The Steven's Point Daily Journal, 28.4.1896
- The Fort Wayne Sentinel, 6.6.1896
- The Steubenville Daily Herald, 28.4.1896
- Marriott, Trevor, Jack the Ripper: The 21st Century Investigation, 2005/2007, John Blake Publishing Ltd
- The Oshkosh Daily Northwestern, 11.4.1890
- Nason, Emma C., Wisconsin – Prostitution & Murder, privately printed, 1893
- The London Times, 26.10.1891

Google Maps for London, USA, Rheinhessen und Pfalz

Website www.familysearch.org on family research in Germany, Great Britain and the USA

Website www.arcinsys.de (Successor to Website www.hadis.hessen.de): Convictions, emigrations in Rheinhessen

Website ofb.genealogy.net (Genealogy Horrweiler)

Website forum.ahnenforschung.net / archive (Genealogy Horrweiler)

Website digiview.gbv.de to ship names at Norddeutschen Lloyd

Website www.casebook.org / suspects / carl-feigenbaum.html to Article by Wolf Vanderlinden on Carl Feigenbaum (alias Anton Zahn from Gau-Bickelheim)

Website forum.casebook.org / to comment by Debra, A., Yorkshire with lists of the crew on ships of Norddeutschen Lloyd from 1872 (Carl Ludwig Zahn, geb. 1853) and 1869 to 1873 (Carl Feigenbaum geb. 1844 in Demmin)

Website books.google.ch / books with the search terms Marriott Trevor Strohband (u.a.)

Website of the newspaper „Rheinhessischer Beobachter" at tudigit.ulb.tu-darmstadt.de /
Jahrgänge 1856 bis 1865 und 1873

Website tv1846alzey.de / geschichte zu Turnvereine

Website www.rhtb.de / gymwelt / zu Turnvereine

Website www.alemania-judaica.de / gau-bickelheim-synagoge. htm zu Population numbers in Gau-Bickelheim, split according to denomination

Website www.ingelheim.de / stadtarchiv-details.html: „Berichtet aus der „Guten alten Zeit" – Ingelheim vor 150 Jahren"

Various websites from www.regionalgeschichte.net about the church in Gau-Bickelheim, Bishop Ketteler etc.

List of Illustrations (on page 192)

Jakob Koeth (1850-1904), detail from the photo where the wedding of my great-grandparents Heinrich Diegel IV and Helena nee Wetzel is celebrated in the farmyard; Summer 1903. (private property)

Johann Otto Hoch (actually: Johann Schmitt or Schmidt) (1855-1906), File: "Johann Otto Hoch.jpg", Foto before 1906, Unknown photographer, detail,
Taken from: https://commons.m.wikimedia.org
License: work "public domain" (engl.) Source:
http://www.executedtoday.com/2012/02/23/1906-johann-otto-hoch-bluebeard/

Carl Ferdinand Feigenbaum (actually: Anton Zahn) (1841-1896), File "zahn10.jpg", graphic from Website https://victorianripper.forumotion.com/t1884-fiegenbaum-was-an.alias, Comment above the graphic: "By telegraph to the Herald", Graphic uploaded by "Karen"

Other illustrations described directly with the pictures

I thank everyone who made the photos available to me.

Translated with www.DeepL.com/Translator (free version)
Up to chapter Markus Adam Nickel & Mary Ann Nichols

Translated with Google Translator
from chapter Disappeared documents onwards

I checked the translations and adjusted them in a few cases.
There may still be several errors in the translation.

Some original english text from Wikipedia is also used.

In my two books in german (2015/2021) there are some more
informations, especially more pictures. If you want, please
look there.

The Pfaffen-Schwabenheim tug-of-war team 1926 in Köln

My grandfather Karl Kolb (1899-1987) (left), trainer of the tug-of-war
team, won in Cologne in 1926 at the fighting games (private property)

1888 house in Pfaffen-Schwabenheim, plan (private), here with the name "J. Köth" instead of "1888"

When I visited London with my parents and brother in 1980, I could not have known that on my mother's side I was apparently so strongly connected to part of the city's history. We were on our way to meet our friends in Nafferton (Yorkshire), who came from Transylvania and the Palatinate, to make a tour of Scotland.

I am also connected to London on my father's side: my father's cousin in Mainz married a diplomat who was the German ambassador to Norway from 1992 to 1996 and the envoy to London from 1988 to 1992. In this role, Helmut Wegner (1931 - 2019) was responsible for organizing the closure of the GDR embassy.

Thomas Hattemer, born 1967 in Bad Kreuznach, grew up in Pfaffen-Schwabenheim, graduated in 1994 with a diploma in physics in Mainz.